METHUEN YOUNG DRAMA

The aim of this series is to offer a range of new plays for children, teen-agers, and young adults. Different volumes present material aimed at different age groups, drawn from the expanding repertoire now being created by a number of modern playwrights and a variety of youth theatres and theatre-in-education companies. Each play is prefaced by an account of the original conception and performance, and suggestions are given for future presentation.

THE INCREDIBLE VANISHING!!!! was written for the Young Vic by Denise Coffey, an actress with the Company, and first performed there in 1973. Intended principally for eight to twelve year olds, the play tells how a barrow boy, a meter maid, and an intrepid police constable descend into the underworld of the Marsh Goblins to investigate an 'incredible vanishing' — the spiriting away of countless children by Her Marshesty, the Monarch of the Drains. Needless to say, our brave heroes (and heroine) save the day — but not without the co-operation of the audience.

This edition includes a Preface by Frank Dunlop, founder and director of the Young Vic, and an Introduction, Production Notes and Music by the author.

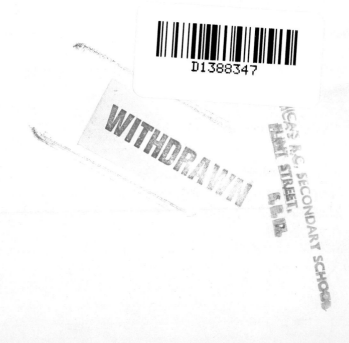

D1388347

WITHDRAWN

...A.C. SECONDARY SCHOOL
FLINT STREET...

in the same series

RECREATIONS
two plays by John Challen
(Pilgrim 70; Transformation Scene)
for 11–14 year olds

THANK YOU VERY MUCH
a play in two acts
by Cecil P Taylor
in collaboration with the
Northumberland Experimental
Youth Theatre

PLAYSPACE
four plays for children by
contemporary writers
(The Cutting of Marchan Wood
by Richard M Hughes;
The Boy without a Head
by Edward Lucie-Smith;
Tamburlane the Mad Hen
by Adrian Mitchell;
The Legend of Scarface and Blue Water
by Niki Marvin)
for 8–14 year-olds

JOHN FORD'S CUBAN MISSILE CRISIS
a play by David Cregan
in collaboration with the
Midlands Arts Centre Repertory
Company
with introductory essays by
David Cregan and Philip Hedley

**THE ADVENTURES OF GERVASE
BECKET**
or The Man Who Changed Places
a play by Peter Terson
originally written for the
Victoria Theatre, Stoke-on-Trent
edited and introduced by
Peter Cheeseman

SNAP OUT OF IT
a programme about mental illness
devised by the Leeds playhouse
Theatre-in-Education Team
edited by Roger Chapman and Brian
Wilks
with an introduction by Brian Wilks

TIMESNEEZE
a play by David Campton
originally written for the
Young Vic Theatre Company

SWEETIE PIE
a play about women in society
devised by the
Bolton Octagon Theatre-in-Education
Company
edited and introduced by
Eileen Murphy

OLD KING COLE
a play by Ken Campbell
originally written for the
Victoria Theatre, Stoke-on-Trent

THE INCREDIBLE VANISHING!!!!

A Play by Denise Coffey

Introduced by Denise Coffey
With a Foreword by Frank Dunlop

First published in Great Britain 1975
by Eyre Methuen Ltd
11 New Fetter Lane, London EC4P 4EE
The Incredible Vanishing!!!!, Introduction,
and Music copyright © 1975 Denise Coffey
Printed in Great Britain by
Whitstable Litho, Straker Brothers Ltd

ISBN 0413 33240 3

CAUTION

*All rights whatsoever in this play are strictly reserved and application for
performance etc should be made before rehearsal to Margaret Ramsay Ltd,
14a Goodwin's Court, London WC2. No performance may be given unless
a licence has been obtained.*

Contents

Acknowledgements (a meagre selection)

J. J. Taylor, C. Rossetti, M. Connelly, W. Shakespeare, P. Roget,
T. S. Eliot, Homer, S. Beckett, Plautus, F. Dunlop, The Beano,
The Dandy, I. Taylor, A. Robertson, G. Reed and The Young
Vic Company.

Foreword

The aim of the Young Vic is to provide the best in theatre for a young audience at a cheap price. Since the theatre opened in 1970, it has attracted a large audience of all ages both at its home base in London and on its many visits to Festivals abroad. The Young Vic production of SCAPINO on Broadway in 1974 followed a season of repertoire at the Brooklyn Academy of Music.

Since 1970 the Young Vic has included in its repertoire eleven productions especially for children:

TIMESNEEZE by David Campton, directed by Roland Joffe.

KING STAG by Carlo Goldoni, English version by Carl Wildman, directed by Roland Joffe.

SYLVESTER AND THE DRAGON (Traditional) directed by Roland Joffe.

THE FANTASTIC FAIRGROUND written and directed by Bernard Goss.

THE SENSATION SEEKERS written and directed by Bernard Goss and the Company.

THE ONLY GOOD INJUN IS A DEAD INJUN! written and directed by Misha Williams.

THE INCREDIBLE VANISHING!!!! written and directed by Denise Coffey (YV actress).

HAMBLEDOG AND THE HOPPING CLOGS by Vivian French, directed by Jeremy James Taylor (YV actor).

THE STATUES IN ROOM 13 by Reg Stewart, directed by Ian Taylor (YV actor).

TOMMY THUMB written and directed by Bernard Goss (YV Associate Director).

THE SPELLBOUND SQUIRE (from Chaucer) written and directed by Jeremy James Taylor.

As a result of our experience with children's audiences, and knowing the lack of plays written especially for children, the Young Vic has now begun to commission plays from its own company. One of the first of these was THE INCREDIBLE VANISHING!!!! by Denise Coffey, created around the Young Vic Company.

Frank Dunlop
Director of the Young Vic

Introduction

THE INCREDIBLE VANISHING!!!! is an entertainment for an audience of children aged eight to twelve, and their parents. The play was commissioned by Frank Dunlop for the Young Vic Theatre and was played there by the company in repertoire in May/June and December/January 1973/4. My thanks to him for his good advice and helpful suggestions — I'd never written for the stage before, only television.

The story of the play (I can't call it a plot) is a mixture of some of the best legends I know, with a basis inspired by Christina Rossetti's extraordinary poem 'Goblin Market', which I first read when I was eight. It stayed with me, and I thought that what had intrigued and frightened me at that age might be likely to affect kids of eight now. 'Goblin Market' starts like this:

Morning and evening
Maids heard the goblins cry:
'Come buy our orchard fruits,
Come buy, come buy:
Apples and quinces,
Lemons and oranges,
Plump unpecked cherries,
Melons and raspberries,
Bloom-down-cheeked peaches,
Swart-headed mulberries,
Wild free-born cranberries,
Crab-apples, dewberries,
Pine-apples, blackberries,
Apricots, strawberries; —
All ripe together
In summer weather, —
Morns that pass by,
Fair eves that fly;
Come buy, come buy:
Our grapes fresh from the vine,
Pomegranates full and fine,
Dates and sharp bullaces,
Rare pears and greengages,
Damsons and bilberries,
Taste them and try:
Currants and gooseberries,
Bright-fire-like barberries,
Figs to fill your mouth,
Citrons from the South,
Sweet to tongue and sound to eye;

Come buy, come buy.'

Evening by evening
Among the brookside rushes,
Laura bowed her head to hear,
Lizzie veiled her blushes:
Crouching close together
In the cooling weather,
With clasping arms and cautioning lips,
With tingling cheeks, and finger tips.
'Lie close,' Laura said,
Pricking up her golden head:
'We must not buy their fruits:
Who knows upon what soil they fed
Their hungry thirsty roots?'
'Come buy,' call the goblins
Hobbling down the glen.
'Oh,' cried Lizzie, 'Laura, Laura,
You should not peep at goblin men.'
Lizzie covered up her eyes,
Covered close lest they should look;
Laura reared her glossy head,
And whispered like the restless brook:
'Look, Lizzie, look, Lizzie,
Down the glen tramp little men.
One hauls a basket,
One bears a plate,
One lugs a golden dish
Of many pounds weight.
How fair the vine must grow
Whose grapes are so luscious;
How warm the wind must blow
Through those fruit bushes.'
'No,' said Lizzie: 'No, no, no;
Their offers should not charm us,
Their evil gifts would harm us.'
She thrust a dimpled finger
In each ear, shut eyes and ran:
Curious Laura chose to linger
Wondering at each merchant man.
One had a cat's face,
One whisked a tail,
One tramped at a rat's pace,
One crawled like a snail,
One like a wombat prowled obtuse and furry,

One like a ratel tumbled hurry skurry.
She heard a voice like voice of doves
Cooing all together:
They sounded kind and full of loves
In the pleasant weather.

The setting of my play is the street in South East London, near Waterloo,
called The Cut (because at one time it was actually a cut, or canal), and
the ancient forgotten kingdom of the Marsh, a mile below the street. It
is in this street, with its lively street market, that the Young Vic Theatre
stands, and the pillar-box of the play stands outside the doors of the
foyer. Although the information in the play about the district is true of
The Cut, it should be taken as being any town or city — most urban
streets have marshes or forgotten rivers somewhere below the surface,
and big pillar-boxes are familiar objects all over the country.

The adventure is basically a collision between two worlds — the upper
and the under . . . in the sense of the upper being the everyday world of
traffic wardens and street markets and the underworld being the place
where the remnants of myths and strange creatures still lurk. Reason and
superstition. Pedestrian precincts and magic kingdoms.

The Marsh Goblins who invade the upperworld should not, under any
circumstances be considered to be endearing in any way. They are
nasty, vicious, dim and noisy and get their comeuppance from their
Monarch, who is even nastier, and more vicious, dim and noisy than
they are.

Our heroes from the upperworld are led by Police Constable Jack
Parker, a handsome, zealous and intelligent young officer (his own
words), who rescues pretty meter maid Jenny Jones from the disgusting
clutches of the wicked Queen of the Underworld by charming the
horrible Monarch with the magic of a transistor radio. (Any resemblance
to the Orpheus legend is deliberate!)

In any traditional adventure story there has to be the Friend of the
Hero, who can be consulted and cajoled, and who can generally assist,
hinder, comment and contribute. Here we have Mr Bert Sparky,
Fruiterer to the Gentry, who is a victim of one series of incredible
vanishings — fruit disappears from his market barrow before his very
eyes!

The Incredible Vanishing of the title can be read about in the programme, which is in the form of a newspaper, The Daily Marsh. Hundreds
of children have disappeared . . . pffffft! . . . just like that! The mystery
reaches the front page of The Daily Marsh. Having a programme in the
form of a newspaper also means that the red spot which is vital to the
play can be contained in the inside pages, together with cartoons and
such like. It's also fun for the kids to have a little newspaper to take
home with them. I noticed a lot of kids in the interval enjoying colouring
in the drawings on the front of our programme. (Programmes are free at

the Young Vic — a commendable practice, and in this case practical too, for every child needs a red spot to hold up to destroy the wicked Queen of the Marshkingdom, which our audiences did with great relish!) But, enough preamble — the text follows, and I hope you enjoy reading it. If you feel tempted to produce the play, there are notes at the end of the text which attempt to offer solutions for some of the practical problems which may occur.

Denise Coffey

THE INCREDIBLE VANISHING!!!! was first presented at the Young Vic Theatre, London SE1, on 18 May 1973 with the following cast:

BERT SPARKY	Gavin Reed
P. C. PARKER	Andrew Robertson
JENNY JONES	Jo Maxwell Muller
LULU MAGUIRE	Jenny Austen
GOB	Ian Charleson
SLURP	Jeremy James Taylor
TWERP	Michael Scholes
H. M.	Ian Taylor
BULK	Alan Coates
ANNOUNCER	Alan Coates

Director: Denise Coffey
Assistant Director: Jeremy James Taylor
Designer: John MacFarlane
Lighting: David Watson
Sound: Marshall Bissett
Stage Manager: Pamela Ross

A BARROW was lent by courtesy of R. Williams, Salad Dealer, The Cut. APPLES were donated by the British Apple and Pear Development Council.

When the play was presented again in December 1973, the part of JENNY JONES was played by Tamara Ustinov, and BUSKERS were introduced. These were played by Ian Taylor, J. James Taylor, Ian Charleson, Michael Scholes, and Alan Coates, and they were led by Hugh Hastings (Pickford Bishop) and Alison Mullin (Mrs Bishop).

The play is in two acts and takes place in a composite set comprising two areas – a deserted city street and the forgotten ancient Kingdom of the Marsh, a mile under the street.

ACT ONE

An empty street. At the edge of the pavement stands a double pillar-box with two slots: one for town, one for country. There has been a light fall of snow.
The six pips which precede the radio news are heard.

ANNOUNCER (over the Public Address system): Here is the news. In the early hours of yesterday afternoon, twenty seven children mysteriously disappeared from the street market, bringing this week's total to three hundred and fifty two. Mothers are reminded to keep their children indoors until the police have solved this mystery of the Incredible Vanishing . . .

(Enter BERT, pushing his barrow and shouting the odds, setting up his stall for the day.)

BERT (roaring): ROSY APPLES JUICY PEARS ORANGES AND LEMONS BELLS OF ST. CLEMENS GET PINEAPPLES HERE AS BIG AS YOUR HEAD LOVELY BLACK GRAPES COCONUTS WALNUTS CHESTNUTS AND PEANUTS: GET YOUR BANANAS ALL YELLOW AND GREEN . . . HERE YOU ARE LADIES THE BEST ONES YOU'VE EVER SEEN GET 'M HERE . . . ROSY APPLES (etc. etc.).

(At exactly the same time as BERT starts shouting, P. C. PARKER'S radio can be heard blaring pop music. Enter P. C. PARKER, engrossed in listening and jiggling to the radio. He collides with BERT's barrow.)

BERT: OI! Watch where you're going . . .

P. C. PARKER: Pardon? (He switches off his radio.)

BERT: WATCH WHERE YOU'RE GOING.

P. C. PARKER: What for? (He switches his radio on again.)

BERT: Charming . . . the whole market's empty but you've got to crash into my barrow.

P. C. PARKER: Do you mind? (He switches his radio off.) You are impeding a Police Officer in the course of his radio listening.

BERT: The police are sending some funny messages these days.

P. C. PARKER: Oh this isn't a police radio, no, mate, that's very boring. Just a lot of yakking about stolen cars and stolen kids and stuff like that . . . this is my radio, much better.

BERT: Oh yes. When are you going to sort out the mystery then? I'm choked with setting up this barrow every day and nobody around to buy anything.

P. C. PARKER: Don't you worry, Mr Sparky . . . I've been put on the case, and I shall bring all my experience in the police force to the assistance of Society.

BERT: How long have you been in the police anyway?

P. C. PARKER: Let's see now . . . one week three days four hours and –

(Looks at his watch.)

– twelve minutes.

BERT: Do me a favour . . . what chance have you got of solving a mystery that's baffled the best brains in Britain?

P. C. PARKER: Relax, Mr Sparky, I'm a policeman who is always on the beat.

(He switches on his radio.)

BERT: I suppose they've got to take what they can get these days. ROSY APPLES RIPE BANANAS GET 'M HERE . . . APPLES A POUND PEARS (etc. etc.).

P. C. PARKER (switching off his radio): 'Allo, 'allo, 'allo.

(He blows his whistle.)

I'm sorry, sir, but I shall have to ask for your name and address.

BERT: What for?

P. C. PARKER: You are creating a disturbance of the peace, and I must warn you that anything you say will be taken down . . .

BERT: Knickers.

P. C. PARKER (writing): Are there two 'R's' in knickers?

BERT: What are you going on about?

P. C. PARKER: Just rehearsing in case I ever make an arrest.

BERT: All right, Sherlock Holmes – here's another mystery for you to solve.

P. C. PARKER: I'm all ears.

BERT: I can see that. How is it that oranges and apples keep disappearing from my barrow when there's nobody around in the market?

P. C. PARKER: I don't know, can I have a question about football please?

BERT: What a genius . . . listen, mate, I'm off to the Goodchild for a cup of tea and a bacon roll . . . if I find any fruit gone when I come back, I'll know who to blame.

(He goes.)

P. C. PARKER: Oh well, he won't need me to solve the mystery.

(He listens to his radio earphone and wanders off half out of sight.)

JENNY & LULU (off-stage): Good morning, Mr Sparky!

BERT (off-stage): Good morning, ladies, nice weather for the time of year.

(If the play is performed at Christmas, or in winter, BERT can say 'Seasonable weather for the time of year'.)

JENNY (off-stage): Morning, Mr Sparky.

LULU (off-stage): I think you're potty, Bert Sparky.

(Enter JENNY JONES and LULU MAGUIRE, traffic wardens, or meter maids if you prefer. LULU is Australian.)

LULU (as they appear): I do, I think he must be potty —

JENNY: Why?

LULU: Nice weather for the time of year — look at it — whoever heard of snow in May?

JENNY: It is unusual.

LULU: Never mind unusual . . . it's dangerous, very slippery, you've got to watch your step or else you're likely to . . . aaaargh!

(She has slipped and fallen.)

(If the play is performed in winter. LULU can say 'Seasonable weather for the time of year! Whoever heard of snow at Christmas — at home we have a heat-wave.' JENNY replies 'It's nice to have snow at Christmas.' and LULU says 'Never mind nice . . . it's dangerous, etc'.)

JENNY: Oh do be careful.

LULU: Don't just stand there, help me up.

JENNY (helping her): Sorry . . . upsadaisy . . .

LULU (grittily): It's all right, I can manage. Oh look at my uniform, all mucky.

JENNY: Bad luck.

LULU: Never mind, I'll be getting a new one as a prize for being the most successful meter maid in Lambeth and District.

JENNY: Congratulations.

LULU: Yes, my parking ticket total this month has reached an all time record of two thousand and seven . . .

(She sees BERT's barrow.)

Two thousand and *eight* . . .

(She puts the ticket on the barrow.)

JENNY: But Mr Sparky's barrow has always stood there.

LULU (smirking unpleasantly): Time it was moved on then, isn't it?

JENNY: But that's not fair.

LULU: What's being fair got to do with it? Listen to me, Jenny Jones,
you'll never be a success unless you seize every opportunity . . .
Remember the traffic wardens' motto: pick a ticket, flick it, stick it.
Look at this book . . . absolutely *full* – I'll have to go back to Headquarters to get a new book, my second today.

JENNY: You mean you've filled a whole book this morning?

LULU: That's right. I was lucky enough to see a traffic jam near Waterloo
Bridge and I got the lot . . . forty five lorries, twenty three buses,
eighty-six cars, twelve motorbikes and two prams . . . nothing escapes
my flying pencil.

JENNY: I've not seen any parked cars today . . .

LULU: What!

JENNY: Well – just one, but the man said he'd broken down, so I
couldn't find it in my heart to give him a parking ticket.

LULU: You didn't *believe* him, did you?

JENNY: Yes.

LULU: That's what they all say . . .

JENNY: Oh!

LULU: Yes, and another thing . . . did I see you putting money into a
parking meter?

JENNY: Yes, poor thing, it hadn't been fed for weeks.

LULU: Sentimental rubbish! No wonder you're going to be fired!

JENNY: Fired?

LULU: Unless you collect more parking tickets today they're going to
tell you to leave . . . didn't you know?

JENNY: No . . .

LULU: Yes . . . Tough potatoes, Jenny . . . you'll never be a success like
Lulu Maguire the champion meter maid 1975.

(The Skaters' Waltz is heard, very loud. P. C. PARKER has been
watching all the time and now skates into view, looking like Raeburn's
skating minister. The music is coming from P. C. PARKER's radio.
The girls join in when he invites them – 'Anyone for skating?')

P. C. PARKER (as they skate): Do you come here often?

LULU: Only in the skating season.

(As they attempt their figure eight, P. C. PARKER stops suddenly, and the girls collide with him. Both fall down, their notebooks flying from their hands. Great screams and shrieks from the girls. P. C. PARKER turns the radio off and picks up a notebook. He looks in the front page, unnoticed by the girls, and hands it to LULU.)

LULU: Oo, thanks P. C. . . .

P. C. PARKER: Parker, Jack Parker.

LULU: Oo, if you're a parker I'd better give you a ticket. (Giggles.) Especially if you're a nosy parker.

P. C. PARKER: Highly humorous, Miss Maguire. You'd better hurry to get that new book — there's a traffic snarl-up near the Strand. Just outside Australia House, I hear.

LULU: Good on ya, Blue! So long, Jenny, don't suppose I'll see you again. Look out for my picture in the papers.

P. C. PARKER: Watch how you go. Remember the snow is very slippy.

LULU (as she goes): All right, don't go on about it, I'm perfectly capable of watching where I'm . . . aaaaaargh.

(Crash of dustbins off-stage. P. C. PARKER laughs, but JENNY is crying.)

P. C. PARKER: Hallo hallo hallo, what's all this?

(He sits on the edge of the pavement beside JENNY.)

JENNY: I'm sorry. (Sniff, sniff.)

P. C. PARKER (giving her a hankie): Come along now, Miss . . . tell me what's the matter.

JENNY (sobbing throughout): Thank you . . . I'm going to have to find another job . . . it's always the same; when I worked in the sweet factory I mixed up the jelly babies with the curly wurlies . . . and when I worked in the supermarket all my pyramids of tins used to collapse . . . and . . . . and when I worked in the launderette I forgot to switch off the driers, and everybody's washing was toasted . . . and now I'm a failure as a Traffic Warden.

P. C. PARKER: There there . . . don't cry . . . I mean, when I think of my first day at work — I have to laugh . . . the mistakes I made!

JENNY: You? But you look so cool!

P. C. PARKER: That's very true. I am. In fact, I'm absolutely frozen.

(He gets up from the snowy step.)

JENNY (getting up too): No, I mean efficient and confident.

P. C. PARKER: Ah, but when I first joined the Police Force two hundred and forty four and a half hours ago, I just couldn't do anything right . . . boots on the wrong feet . . . had no idea what the time was when asked . . . and even arrested a man for climbing in a first floor window.

JENNY: Well, that doesn't sound like a mistake.

P. C. PARKER: He was a window cleaner.

JENNY: Oh.

P. C. PARKER: Everybody makes mistakes sometimes.

JENNY: Lulu Maguire doesn't.

P. C. PARKER: Is that a fact . . . ? Is this your notebook?

JENNY: Thanks.

P. C. PARKER: Just have a look inside –

JENNY: What for, it's . . . oo! It's full of parking numbers!

P. C. PARKER: Look in the front page.

JENNY (reading): If this book should chance to roam, smack its bot and send it home to: Lulu Maguire, 5 Railway Buildings, London, Britain, Europe, The Western Hemisphere, The World, The Universe, Space, Infinity . . . This isn't my book!

P. C. PARKER: With a brain like that you should be in the police force!

JENNY: But –

P. C. PARKER: Miss Maguire must have taken your book, mustn't she?

JENNY: Yes.

P. C. PARKER: That's a very bad thing to do, isn't it?

JENNY: Yes!

P. C. PARKER: She's lucky that you found her book, isn't she?

JENNY: Yes!

P. C. PARKER: It's the worst crime a Traffic Warden can commit, isn't it?

JENNY: Yes!

P. C. PARKER: To lose her book.

JENNY: Yes!

P. C. PARKER: To lose her book?

JENNY: Yes!

P. C. PARKER: Well then, you won't be asked to leave now, will you?

JENNY: Yes – No – Why not?

P. C. PARKER: You've saved all those parking tickets from being lost, haven't you?

JENNY: Well, yes, I suppose I have —

P. C. PARKER: In fact, you are a success, aren't you?

JENNY: Yes, I suppose I am . . . wasn't it lucky she went off with the wrong book?

P. C. PARKER: Very lucky.

(BERT rushes back in, shouting very loudly. He is carrying a cup of tea.)

BERT: Right ! Drop 'em . . . I know you've got them. Drop them, come on now, turn out your pockets or I'll get the Police.

(He sees JENNY and P. C. PARKER.)

Oh. It's you.

P. C. PARKER: What's the matter, Mr Sparky?

BERT: Just checking that you're keeping an eye on my barrow . . . (Looking at the fruit.) Let's see . . . yes, they all seem to be here. I just don't understand it — when I'm *not* here none of the fruit is stolen, and when I *am* here, oranges and apples vanish before my very eyes.

JENNY: But who can take it? There's nobody in the street these days.

BERT: I know . . . I'm fed up with all this . . . why can't everything be like the good old days three months ago. (Sings.)

<u>MARKET SONG*</u>
I wish it was three months ago
When there wasn't any nasty slippy slidy snow.
Children everywhere . . .

P. C. PARKER & JENNY: Ya-ta-ta ta.

BERT: And the noises of the market in the air. There
Was Henry and his fish barrow
Standing over there.

P. C. PARKER: Ah yes, the memory lingers on . . .

(P. C. PARKER and JENNY sniff like Bisto kids.)

BERT: Fine fat haddocks, juicy kippers,
New caught herring . . .

P. C. PARKER: They're good for the nippers.

BERT (pointing): There was Bill the rag and bone man —

JENNY & P. C. PARKER (pointing to a different spot): And
Fred the hot pie stall —

*The Music for all the songs appears on p. 73.

P. C. PARKER: And —

(P. C. PARKER and BERT point at JENNY.)

— Violet Puke the flower-seller,
Sweetest of them all.

JENNY: Daffodils, marigolds, sixpence a bunch . . .

BERT & P. C. PARKER: Back in five minutes, I've gone for me lunch.

ALL THREE: In the good old days three months ago . . .

VOICE OF RAG 'N' BONE MAN: *Ragabones, any old iron!*

ALL THREE: When there wasn't any nasty slippy slidy snow . . .

VOICE OF PIE-SELLER: *Juicy hot pies fresh from the oven!*

VOICE OF OLD CLOTHES WOMAN: *There's lovely old socks a penny a dozen!*

ALL THREE: Children everywhere . . . .

VOICE OF COBBLER: *Shoes to mend!*

ALL THREE: And the noises of the market in the air — ooh!

VOICE OF RAG 'N' BONE MAN:	*Ragabones any old iron!*
VOICE OF PIE-SELLER:	*Juicy hot pies fresh from the oven!*
VOICE OF RAG 'N' BONE MAN:	*Ragabones any old iron!*
VOICE OF OLD CLOTHES WOMAN:	*Lovely old socks a penny a dozen!*
VOICE OF PIE-SELLER:	*Juicy hot pies fresh from the oven!*
VOICE OF RAG 'N' BONE MAN:	*Ragabones any old iron!*
VOICE OF COBBLER:	*Shoes to mend boots to heel!*
VOICE OF OLD CLOTHES WOMAN:	*Lovely old socks a penny a dozen!*
VOICE OF PIE-SELLER:	*Juicy hot pies fresh from the oven!*
VOICE OF RAG 'N' BONE MAN:	*Ragabones any old iron!*

JENNY, BERT & P. C. PARKER: And the jets from all parts of the world in the sky . . .

(VOICES make jet noises.)

JENNY, BERT & P. C. PARKER: And the kids in the school let out to play . . .

(VOICES sing 'La-la-la-la-la-lah-lah' to Ring-a-ring-a-roses tune.)

JENNY, BERT & P. C. PARKER: And the people out shopping a-spending their pay . . .

(VOICES go 'Ca-Ching!' like a cash till.)

JENNY, BERT & P. C. PARKER: And the beautiful beautiful traffic . . .

(VOICES make beeping and hooting noises.)

JENNY, BERT & P. C. PARKER: A roaring and a hooting and a parking all day.

VOICES:	JENNY, BERT & P. C. PARKER:
Ragabones any old iron!	A jetting and a betting
	And a selling
Pick a ticket, flick it, stick it!	And a smelling
	And a crying and a frying
	And a spending and a mending
Shoes to mend boots to heel!	And a vending and a sending
	And a touting and a shouting –
Aaah!	Aaah!

BERT: And now there's only me, crying: 'APPLES A POUND PEARS . . .'

(He is interrupted by the radio, playing Cliff Richard's *Power to all our friends*.)

Oh shut up with that row.

(P. C. PARKER turns the radio off.)

P. C. PARKER: I'm listening for the news.

(He turns the radio on again.)

ANNOUNCER (on radio): Here is the news.

JENNY: See!

ANNOUNCER: Although no more children are reported missing from the market, there is no sign of the three hundred and fifty two children who have already vanished. 'We are baffled,' say the police . . .

BERT (writing a birthday card): They're not the only ones, mate.

ANNOUNCER: Home News: Miss Lulu Maguire, a Traffic Warden who was to have been awarded the Meter Maid of the Year prize, has been disqualified for losing her parking book.

(JENNY, P. C. PARKER and BERT cheer.)

'I don't understand it,' she said at her Railway Buildings home today . . . 'There is something very funny going on in the market'.

BERT: You can say that again.

ANNOUNCER (repeating himself exactly): There is something very funny going ón in the market.

JENNY: It's not funny, it's mysterious.

(P. C. PARKER turns the radio off.)

P. C. PARKER: Well, at least nothing more mysterious can happen.

BERT (going to the pillar-box): It had better not, that's all – with all this uproar I nearly forgot to post this birthday card to Auntie Ethel.

(He posts it in one slot, and it is spat out of the other slot.)

JENNY: Oo look, the pillar-box is being sick.

P. C. PARKER: Can't have been a very nice birthday card, Mr Sparky.

BERT: Must have been, it cost 12p plus VAT.

JENNY: I'll post it for you —

(She looks at the box and the card. Then as she posts it, she sings:)

Happy Birthday, Auntie Ethel.

ALL (singing): Happy Birthday to you!

(The pillar-box spits the card out again.)

P. C. PARKER: Excuse me, while I investigate this problem.

(He posts the card, putting his hand right into the slot.)

Now then, that card is well and truly posted . . . Ouch!

BERT: What's up?

JENNY: What's the matter?

P. C. PARKER: My hand . . . it's trapped . . . something's clutching my fingers . . .

(The card pops out of the other slot. P. C. PARKER tries to get free, then suddenly falls.)

JENNY: Do be careful, Mr Parker . . .

BERT: What are you messing about at, Officer?

P. C. PARKER: Ow . . .

(He speaks into the pillar-box.)

What's going on here?

BERT: Here's Auntie Ethel's birthday card again . . . I think I'll send it by pigeon.

JENNY: Are you all right, Mr Parker?

P. C. PARKER (looking into the pillar-box with a torch): That's very strange . . .

JENNY: What is?

P. C. PARKER: This pillar-box is empty, but my hand was definitely grabbed, and I thought I heard . . .

JENNY & BERT: Yes?

P. C. PARKER: Well, what we in the police force have learned to identify as nasty sniggering!

BERT: Your brain's turned with listening to that radio all day long. Nasty sniggering, indeed. I ask you, what next?

P. C. PARKER: Exactly, what next!

JENNY: It's frightening.

BERT: I'm not frightened! Well, I'm going to post this card down the Post Office. Watch my barrow, won't be long . . . (BERT goes hastily.)

P. C. PARKER: Bring us back a cup of tea . . .

BERT (off-stage): Right . . .

JENNY: Mr Sparky's frightened too.

P. C. PARKER: I'm not feeling too brave myself.

JENNY: Let's be sensible about this. There must be *some* reasonable answer to all these strange happenings.

P. C. PARKER: Yes, of course there must be . . . in fact, something very like this happened hundreds of years ago — children vanishing, mysterious events of all sorts, unseasonable weather . . .

(He can allude to any topical or local event, e.g. England out of the World Cup.)

JENNY: How do you know that?

P. C. PARKER: There's a book in the library about this district as it was many centuries ago . . . and the street where we're walking used to be a canal which had windmills beside it . . .

JENNY: There's a pub called the Windmill down the road.

P. C. PARKER: Yes, that really used to be a windmill . . . but here, where we are, there was a marsh, a really horrible place by all accounts —

(A shrill and discordant whistling begins — The Theme of the Marsh-goblins.)

nothing grew here but water weeds and twisted trees with roots like snakes . . . travellers never ventured near the marsh at night for fear of . . .

(The pillar-box door opens and shuts.)

JENNY: Of what?

P. C. PARKER: Of being lost and led astray across the bogs and swamps by the strange light called will o' the wisp . . . led into the dreaded Kingdom of the Marsh Goblins . . . from which they *never* returned.

JENNY: How creepy . . . but that was hundreds of years ago, wasn't it?

P. C. PARKER: Yes, but the marsh is there still, under the street . . . way down below the telephone cables and the gas mains and the drains and the tube trains, and if the marsh is there still, maybe the Goblins are too.

JENNY: But, Mr Parker, people nowadays don't believe in Goblins . . . there's no such thing . . . as a Goblin . . . is there?

(BERT returns in time to hear about the GOBLINS. He is carrying three cups of tea.)

BERT: 'Course there's not.

(JENNY and P. C. PARKER jump in fright.)

Lot of rubbish, stupid fairy stories . . . Come and get your tea . . .

JENNY: Oh, you gave me a fright!

BERT: I'm not the one giving people frights . . . what about helmet there, with those daft stories about Marsh Goblins.

P. C. PARKER: Well, Mr Sparky, over the years people have claimed to see them.

BERT: At closing time I wouldn't wonder . . . come and get your tea.

(P. C. PARKER and JENNY follow him over to the barrow. He sees the parking ticket.)

Hallo, Lulu Maguire's been here. She'd have her own grandmother towed away, that one. Still, come in handy when I start the confetti factory.

(He tears the ticket to shreds and throws the pieces in the air.)

JENNY: What did they look like, the Marsh Goblins?

P. C. PARKER: Well, the identikit picture I have assembled shows them to be approximately human height but with very pointed ears.

BERT: Do me a favour . . . who'd believe in things like that?

(The pillar-box opens and a MARSH GOBLIN emerges, exactly as described, except that he wears a boiler suit. His hands are seen to be leathery and his ears very pointed. He blinks in the direction of the barrow.)

JENNY: Hasn't it gone cold suddenly.

(P. C. PARKER and BERT agree. They all drink their tea, and BERT reads his paper. GOB looks into the pillar-box and shouts.)

GOB: Get a move on — we haven't got all day.

SLURP (from inside the pillar-box): All right, all right, keep your ears on.

(SLURP, another Marsh Goblin, hands out a small barrow, and comes out himself. Sings to the tune of 'Underneath the Arches':)

Underneath the marshes, I dream my dreams away . . .

GOB: Shuttup, Slurp. No time for singing.

SLURP: Ooops, sorry gaffer Gob.

(SLURP shuts the door of the pillar-box and catches the hand of TWERP, a third Marsh Goblin, who is following.)

TWERP: Oooooooow!

(He pushes open the door and comes out, still squawking.)

SLURP: Shuttup, Twerp. No time for singing.

TWERP: Sorry.

(He shuts pillar-box door.)

Ooh, it's very bright in the Upper World.

GOB: Put on your Upper World Eyelids.

SLURP: Upper World Eyelids – Ready –

GOB: Steady –

ALL: On!

(They put on dark glasses – in unison.)

TWERP (looking round, spots P. C. PARKER, BERT and JENNY): Ah! Children! Hallo there! Yoohoo! We're coming to get you! They didn't take any notice of me, what's the matter with them?

SLURP: Anybody can see that this is your first visit to the Upper World . . . we are invisible to humans.

GOB: Until we choose to become visible, that is.

TWERP: How do we do that, gaffer Gob?

GOB: Didn't you listen to anything I told you on the journey?

TWERP: No.

SLURP (tweaking his ear): No wonder you've been a learner for two hundred years . . . when we want to be seen and heard we put on our human head-lids.

TWERP: Oh . . . like this, you mean?

(He puts on a bowler hat. GOB and SLURP leap on him and snatch it off.)

GOB & SLURP: Not yet, you dope!

BERT: Blimey!

JENNY & P. C. PARKER: What?

BERT: I thought I saw a . . .

P. C. PARKER: A what?

BERT: Eh? Oh . . . nothing.

P. C. PARKER: Nobody can see *nothing* . . .

JENNY: It's not there.

TWERP: What did I do wrong? I only put on this . . .

> (He puts the hat on again.)

GOB & SLURP (grabbing it off him): Will you stop doing that!

BERT (choking on his tea): There it is again . . .

P. C. PARKER: What?

BERT: Oh . . . nothing, must remember to get my eyes tested.

GOB (blows a whistle): Goblins, pay attention. We all know what we must do.

SLURP: Yes, yes.

TWERP: No, I don't know what we must do.

> (GOB hits TWERP. SLURP wheels their barrow forward.)

GOB: See that barrow?

TWERP: Yes.

SLURP: What's in it?

TWERP: The inside.

GOB: That's right. We must fill it —

> (Hits TWERP.)

> — with oranges and apples . . .

SLURP: Which we enchant . . .

GOB: With Marsh fire . . .

SLURP: And we give them to children.

GOB: And we lure them back to the Kingdom under the Marsh.

SLURP: From which they never, never, never return.

> (GOB hits TWERP.)

GOB: Goblins, ready — steady — steal!

> (The GOBLINS take up stealing positions. Meanwhile, JENNY has dropped her pencil. She has been doing the crossword in BERT's paper.)

P. C. PARKER: Oh look, you've dropped your pencil!

BERT: And my paper!

> (As they all bend down to retrieve the paper and pencil, SLURP creeps up behind them and pinches them.)

JENNY: Stop being silly.

BERT: Stop being silly yourself.

P. C. PARKER: Can that have been a wasp I ask myself?

(The GOBLINS steal fruit — two oranges and one apple — calling out like acrobats: "Hup — hup — hup — bonk". The thrower shouts 'Hup!' as he throws, and the final 'Bonk' is the fruit landing in the GOBLINS' barrow. If any fruit is inadvertently dropped, the failed catcher shouts 'Splat!')

BERT: Oi! LOOK LOOK — It's happening again.

JENNY & P. C. PARKER: What what?

BERT: Look — oranges and apples disappearing off of me barrow before me very eyes!

(JENNY and P. C. PARKER watch BERT's barrow closely.)

JENNY: Looks all right to me.

P. C. PARKER: I can't see oranges and apples disappearing.

BERT: Of course you can't — they've vanished.

JENNY: I don't understand any of that.

P. C. PARKER: Neither do I.

(GOB and TWERP march past the barrow, and SLURP fills their bowler hats with fruit. Then SLURP carries a bunch of three bananas over to GOB and TWERP: BERT sees the bananas pass in front of his nose.)

BERT (hysterically): Bananas!

JENNY & P. C. PARKER: Pardon?

BERT: Bananas . . . flying through the air.

JENNY & P. C. PARKER: Where?

BERT: They've gone now.

P. C. PARKER (taking out his notebook): I see, sir . . .

(The GOBLINS are eating the bananas.)

Could you describe these bananas?

BERT: Well . . . sort of yellow and . . . you know what a banana looks like.

P. C. PARKER: And what exactly were these bananas doing?

BERT: They were flying . . .

P. C. PARKER: Flying . . .

BERT: Through the air.

P. C. PARKER: Would you say they were hurtling . . . or whizzing . . . or perhaps describing a graceful arc?

JENNY: What a beautiful speaker!

P. C. PARKER: Thank you.

BERT: They were just . . . flying . . . through the air.

P. C. PARKER: Then what did they do?

BERT: They vanished.

P. C. PARKER: Vanished? With a loud explosion of any sort . . . a bang . . . a whimper?

JENNY: Sheer poetry.

P. C. PARKER: Thank you.

BERT (head in hands): No, they just . . . vanished.

(The GOBLINS throw the banana skins back to TWERP, who puts them into BERT's outstretched hand.)

They were here . . . Aaaargh! They're back!

P. C. PARKER: Aha!

BERT: But they're empty!

P. C. PARKER: Oho!

JENNY: Empty?

P. C. PARKER: So you wish to report the theft of the contents of three bananas.

BERT: Yes, I suppose I do.

JENNY: Lulu Maguire's quite right, Mr Sparky . . . you're potty.

BERT: No I'm not . . . Look, I'll prove to you that oranges and apples are vanishing . . .

JENNY: Go on then.

(BERT takes a felt-tip pen and draws faces on the oranges and apples.)

BERT: There, see? Clearly marked with a face.

P. C. PARKER: Identifruit.

JENNY: Can I do one?

BERT: Help yourself.

JENNY (having drawn a face on an apple): Who's this?

P. C. PARKER: I don't know, who is it?

JENNY: Granny Smith! (She falls about.)

P. C. PARKER (having drawn a face on an orange): Who's this?

JENNY: I don't know, who is it?

P. C. PARKER: William of Orange. (He falls about.)

(The GOBLINS collect more fruit: SLURP fills first GOB's hat, then TWERP's hat, and finally takes the orange out of BERT's hand. All the GOBLINS return to their barrow.)

BERT (as the orange is taken from his hand): Oooh!

P. C. PARKER: Calm down, Mr Sparky. Here read your horoscope, that'll cheer you up.

BERT: There's no future in that.

(The GOBLINS gather round and TWERP and SLURP whistle the Theme of the Marshgoblins, as they all sprinkle the Marsh Goblin glitter on the fruit by waving sparklers over it.)

THE THEME OF THE MARSHGOBLINS

GOB (speaking over the whistling):
Dust from the dead Moon
Glitter from an evil star
Light to lead travellers astray
To the kingdom where Marsh Goblins are . . .
Turn red and gold to cinders
Taste sweet in the mouth
But burn in the brain
Whoever eats this enchanted fruit
Will never be seen on earth again.

Ho Ho Ho Ho

Will never be seen on earth again.

(The GOBLINS look beadily at the three.)

JENNY: This orange looks a bit like you, P. C. Parker.

P. C. PARKER: This rosy apple is as pretty as you, Miss Jones.

BERT: Concentrate, will you . . . watch this barrow very very closely.

(They all stare fixedly at BERT's barrow. GOB whistles.)

GOB: Prepare to search for children. Ready – steady – wait for it! – APPEAR!

TWERP: Hallo.

BERT: Hallo.

GOB: Hallo.

JENNY: Hallo.

SLURP: Hallo.

P. C. PARKER: Hallo hallo hallo . . .

SLURP: Sweet fruit for children to sink their white teeth in.

TWERP: Golden oranges with sunshine from far far away.

SLURP: Red rosy apples taste one today.

BERT: Oi, clear off, this is my pitch.

TWERP: Sweet as honey and bitter as gall.

SLURP: Plenty to buy.

TWERP & SLURP: Come one come all.

BERT: Oi, officer . . .

P. C. PARKER: Yes?

BERT: P. C. Parker . . . move this lot on, they're spoiling my trade.

P. C. PARKER: What trade — there's nobody here, is there?

BERT: I know, but if there was, they would be.

JENNY: Please don't start confusing us again, Mr Sparky . . . How much are your oranges?

BERT: Beautiful oranges only five pence each . . . three for twelve, special sale price, buy 'm here.

TWERP: Try our golden globes, glittering with juice . . .

SLURP: Only three brown pennies — any one you choose.

JENNY: Oo . . .

P. C. PARKER: That seems a bargain . . .

BERT (roaring): All right, I tell you what I'll do . . . five pence to anyone else . . . two pence to you . . . .

JENNY: Mm . . .

P. C. PARKER: Can't say fairer than that.

TWERP: Rosy red apples warm from the tree . . . Picked from an orchard within sound of the sea . . .

TWERP & SLURP: Absolutely freeeeee.

JENNY: Oh what a promise!

P. C. PARKER: What an offer.

BERT: What a liberty! (Roaring.) A pound of apples and a pound of pears . . . lemons and oranges, peaches and plums . . . good for the kids and good for their mums . . . twenty pence the lot.

JENNY: Right . . . it's a deal.

SLURP: Before you buy . . .

TWERP: Why not try . . .

TWERP & SLURP: This extra special orange.

(They hand her an orange. The Marshgoblins theme is heard briefly.)

JENNY: What a beautiful orange . . .

P. C. PARKER: It seems to be glowing . . .

GOB: Excuse us if we disappear for a moment.

(The GOBLINS take their hats off.)

JENNY & BERT: Oo, where are they?

P. C. PARKER: *I* don't know!

GOB (tweaking their ears): You idiot goblins, we must steal only CHILDREN . . . that one's not a child . . . we must get that orange back. Ready, steady, APPEAR.

(They put their hats on.)

JENNY: Ah, there you are. I'd like this orange, please.

GOB: Very well – That'll be five hundred pounds.

P. C. PARKER: What?

JENNY: That's a big price increase.

BERT: Told you they were Common Marketeers.

GOB: It's the cost of living, it's gone up suddenly.

P. C. PARKER: It certainly has!

GOB: Five hundred pounds.

JENNY: That's a bit expensive . . . perhaps I won't try the orange after all

(Gives them back the orange.)

GOBLINS (sighing with relief): Whew!

JENNY: I'll have an apple instead.

GOBLINS (panic-stricken): That'll be eight hundred pounds . . .

TWERP: At least.

SLURP: That's right.

P. C. PARKER: It must be a golden delicious.

JENNY: What a disappointment, they looked so pretty . . .

BERT: Oi, why don't you buy from my barrow . . . top quality fruit at best prices.

GOB: That's a good idea.

SLURP: Yes yes, buy from him, lovely oranges.

TWERP: Beautiful red apples.

BERT: You've changed your tune . . . got some sense in you at last, eh?

They're quite right, buy from me.

(BERT and the GOBLINS all shout their wares together − chaos.)

P. C. PARKER (blows his whistle): That's enough of that . . . you lot, back to your barrows, and listen to me . . . Now then, if the young lady wants to buy an apple, she should be allowed to buy an apple at the right price from the barrow of her choice.

BERT: Wait a minute−
JENNY: Oh but I −
TWERP: No but −   (In confused unison.)
SLURP: It's got to −
GOB: You don't under −

P. C. PARKER (blows his whistle): Silence.

(They all look as if they're about to start again. But P. C. PARKER blows his whistle like a referee and holds up his hand like a traffic stop. They shut up abruptly. He lowers his hand and they start again immediately. P. C. PARKER raises his hand and they stop even more abruptly.)

(To the GOBLINS.) You offered this young lady a red apple absolutely freeeee according to my notes.

GOBLINS: Yes but . . .

P. C. PARKER: If you make a promise like that, then you have to keep it.

GOBLINS: Ooooo but . . .

P. C. PARKER: Therefore . . . According to the law of supply and demand . . .

(He takes an apple from the GOBLINS' barrow.)

Here you are, Miss Jones, there's a lovely red apple for you . . .

JENNY: Oh, thank you, it's beautiful.

P. C. PARKER: And here's five pence for one of your bananas, Bert, so everybody's happy.

BERT: Ta.

P. C. PARKER (saluting): Happy to be of service.

JENNY: It's so tempting . . . I think I'll eat it now.

GOBLINS: Oooooooooooo! (They retreat, cringing, with their barrow.)

(JENNY bites into the apple.)

JENNY: Mmmm it's lovely and juicy . . . what a . . . oh!

(Whistling − the Theme of the Marshgoblins − is heard very loudly, fading over the following speeches and ending when the pillar-box door clangs shut.)

P. C. PARKER: What's the matter?

JENNY: The street . . . it's disappeared . . . where's the street?

P. C. PARKER: Under the snow.

BERT: What's up with her?

JENNY: Black water as far as the eye can see . . . and look at those water weeds and twisted trees with roots like snakes . . .

P. C. PARKER: Jenny . . .

JENNY: And it's getting so dark . . . I'll never reach the windmill across the swamp . . . P. C. Parker, where are you?

P. C. PARKER (beside her): I'm here, Jenny, where are you?

JENNY: Bert! Mr Sparky, where are you?

BERT: I'm here, Jenny . . .

JENNY: It's so frightening alone in this horrible marsh . . . Help! Help!

P. C. PARKER: It's all right, Jenny – here we are.

JENNY: Oh thank goodness . . . look, a light in the distance . . . (The pillar-box is glowing.) I must go to the light, to the beautiful Kingdom of the Goblins . . .

P. C. PARKER: No, no, Jenny, stay here . . .

A DISTANT VOICE: Jenny Jones! Jenny Jones!

JENNY (heading for the pillar-box): I hear sweet music and voices calling to me.

BERT: There's no music, no voices . . .

JENNY: Follow the glowing light . . . to the land of sweet delight . . . to the Kingdom of the Goblins . . . where the day is always night . . . That's where I want to be, and never, never, never return . . .

(The door of the pillar-box has swung open and JENNY goes in. Inside there is a greenish light. The door clangs shut behind her. Everyone is galvanised into action. The GOBLINS, BERT and P. C. PARKER all collide with each other in a terrible rush.)

P. C. PARKER: Jenny! Come back . . .

GOB: Grab that apple!

BERT: Oi, where has she gone?

GOB: Let's get out of here.

(They sort themselves out. P. C. PARKER rushes to the pillar-box. It's locked.)

BERT: What's going on here?

GOB: Ready steady . . .

P. C. PARKER: Just a minute, you three . . . I've got some questions to ask you . . .

GOB: VANISH!!!

P. C. PARKER: Get them!

(The GOBLINS take off their hats. They manage to heave their barrow to the pillar-box. P. C. PARKER and BERT collide in a bear hug, having been rushing towards the GOBLINS, who stood between them. The pillar-box opens. The GOBLINS clamber in in disorder. Meanwhile, BERT and P. C. PARKER are hunting for them, P. C. PARKER blowing his whistle.)

BERT: Where have they gone? They must be here somewhere . . .

P. C. PARKER: Come out, wherever you are . . .

BERT: I knew there was something funny about those fellas . . .

P. C. PARKER: If we can find them, we may be able to find Jenny . . .

(They ad lib their hunting and shouting as much as is needed, avoiding the invisible GOBLINS climbing into the pillar-box with their barrow. When they are inside, P. C. PARKER spies the door open.)

Look, Bert . . . the pillar-box is open again . . . STOP in the name of the Law!

(An orange, dropped by the GOBLINS in their haste, rolls out of the pillar-box and lies on the ground.)

(Getting into the pillar-box.) I know you're . . . oh, there's a tunnel. I'm going to follow them.

BERT: Oi . . . this is one of my oranges . . . it's got a face on it. (Going back to his barrow.) Look, like this one . . . P. C. Parker . . .

(BERT gets into the pillar-box with both oranges.)

(Voice disappearing.) Oi . . . P. C. Parker . . . They're the ones who stole my oranges . . . coo, it's dark down here . . .

(The lights fade on the street area and come up dimly on the cavern area. Various sounds are heard: P. C. PARKER shouting 'Jenny – where are you?' The GOBLINS shouting 'Quick, get a move on', and 'I've fallen in the water'; children crying; water rushing; BERT shouting 'P. C. Parker . . . where are you?' JENNY emerges into the Cavern.)

JENNY: What a beautiful place . . . what beautiful music I hear. What beautiful flowers!

(From the dark the sound of children crying.)

P. C. PARKER (from the dark): Jenny, where are you?

BERT (from the dark): Oi . . . give us a hand to get out of this drain . . . Where are we, Waterloo Station?

P. C. PARKER (shining his torch around): What a huge cavern! We must be at least a mile under the street.

BERT (pointing down one aisle): Look, here's a tunnel − I wonder where it leads?

P. C. PARKER (pointing down another aisle): Here's another tunnel.

BERT: It's like Oxford Circus, never mind Waterloo Station.

P. C. PARKER (at steps): Well anyway, we'll be all right if we need to take the necessary steps.

BERT: Stop messing about, we're looking for Jenny Jones, remember?

JENNY (sings to the tune of 'Beautiful Dreamer'): Beautiful Kingdom under the Marsh . . .

BERT: There she is!

P. C. PARKER: Jenny! Thank goodness!

JENNY: Who are you? Go away, you're ugly.

P. C. PARKER: Jenny!

BERT: Ugh! What a smell!

JENNY (sniffing): Summer evening breeze from a flowery meadow, sunshine and seaside and fresh bread baking . . .

BERT (sniffing): More like winter morning drizzle and diesel oil spilling . . .

P. C. PARKER: And gasworks and old rags and cabbage stalks burning.

JENNY: Oh look, isn't it sweet!

P. C. PARKER: What's she pointing at?

BERT: Aaaargh, it's a rat . . .

(P. C. PARKER follows it under the feet of the audience with his torch.)

P. C. PARKER: There it goes . . .

BERT: It's a big one . . .

JENNY: Pretty rat . . .

P. C. PARKER: Wicked red eyes . . .

(Tracks it down and smashes it with the torch.)

Got it!

BERT: Be careful, it'll bite you!

P. C. PARKER: Ugh . . . it's only an old sock swirling round the sewers . . .

(The GOBLINS arrive, quarrelling. They have kazoos round their necks on strings.)

GOB: How could you get lost, you fools . . .

SLURP: I was following you.

TWERP: I was following you.

GOB: Shuttup. READY! STEADY! — APPEAR!

(Hats on.)

P. C. PARKER & BERT: AHA!

GOBLINS: OHO!

(P. C. PARKER blows his whistle. He and BERT pounce.)

BERT: You stole my oranges — I'm going to bash you . . .

P. C. PARKER (blows his whistle): I must warn you
that anything you say may be taken down and   (All three speaking
used in evidence against you.   at once.)
TWERP: We don't want you to be here.
SLURP: Go away, please . . .

(General bashing, squealing and uproar. Suddenly they hear a metallic voice from above.)

VOICE: STOP THAT AT ONCE.

(Everybody freezes and looks towards the source of the voice.)

GOBLINS (whimpering): SOMEBODY VERY IMPORTANT!

VOICE: Stand still. Everybody stay exactly where they are!

ANNOUNCER'S VOICE: The voice belongs to . . . Somebody Very Important . . . The Queen of the Marshgoblins . . . Her Marshesty in person.

(The GOBLINS play 'Tara!' on their Kazoos.)

The most evil and dangerous monarch in existence today . . .

(Fanfare on Kazoos and National Anthem, as HER MARSHESTY makes her way to the Cavern by the most spectacular route available. She carries an old-fashioned megaphone through which she speaks orders, or shrieks when emphasizing a point. In her other hand she carries a loofah, useful for hitting people.)

<u>THE MARSHELLAISE</u>
GOBLINS (sing):
    Squelch squelch squelch

    Here comes the Queen.
    Squelch squelch squelch
    She's really mean.
    Sludge and mud and seeping oil,
    Rotting leaves, polluted soil
    Is the diet of this Royal . . .
    People cringe as she goes by . . .
    Perish crumble putrefy . . .
    SQUELCH SQUELCH SQUELCH

P. C. PARKER: What's that song?

GOB: It's our National Anthem — The Marshellaise.

    (The Marshellaise is played again, very fast.)

H.M.: Thank you!

    (All stop except a distant kazoo.)

    And you!

    (It dwindles to a stop. H. M. arrives in the cavern. The GOBLINS cringe and shout loyally.)

GOB: Gob slave Your Marshesty! SQUELCH SQUELCH SQUELCH.

SLURP: SLURP SLURP SLURP . . . May Your Marshesty moulder for ever . . .

TWERP: TODAY! TOADY! TOADY! Simper! Simper!

H. M.: All right, that's quite enough of that . . . Shuttup. (Hits them.)

GOBLINS: Thank you thank you.

JENNY: What a beautiful gracious lady . . .

BERT: You're joking . . .

P. C. PARKER: What's that horrible smell?

H. M.: You like my perfume? It's Canal number 5.

P. C. PARKER: Ugh! Smells like burnt feathers and bad eggs.

H. M.: That's right, what an intelligent child.

GOBLINS: Um er . . . Your Marshesty . . . this isn't . . .

H. M.: What are you yakking about — THRONE!

    (The GOBLINS form themselves into a throne: one GOBLIN goes onto all fours for the seat; the other two stand behind him with their arms round each other, and holding their other arms as arms for the 'throne'.)

H. M. (sitting down): Now then, let's have a look at you.

BERT: What for?

H. M.: You've got a deep voice for a tiny tot.

BERT: Eh?

GOBLINS: Ooh?

H. M.: And look at these other children . . . they're very *large* —

GOBLINS: Ooooooo!

H. M.: What's the matter with them? Look at their heads . . .

GOBLINS: Ooooo!

P. C. PARKER: I beg your pardon?

JENNY: Don't interrupt the beautiful lady . . . her voice is like sweet music.

H. M. (pointing at BERT): That one's got a flat head —

(P. C. PARKER laughs at BERT.)

— and (Pointing at JENNY.) that one's got a yellow stripe around its head, and (Pointing at P. C. PARKER.) that one's ridiculous . . .

P. C. PARKER: Excuse me, madam . . .

H. M.: That's all right, you can't help it . . . any gnomes in your family by any chance?

P. C. PARKER: I must warn you, madam . . .

GOBLINS: Ooooooo!

H. M.: Listen, pointed head, don't call me Madam . . . I am to be addressed at all times as Your Marshesty, unless you happen to be a friend of mine, which in this case you *don't* happen to be, in which case you would call me Smarm or for really informal festive occasions I answer to the title of Sewer High Royalness.

P. C. PARKER: . . . Very well, I must warn you that anything you say will be taken down in writing and may be used in evidence.

H. M.: Antidisestablishmentarianism.

P. C. PARKER: Anything you say after this will be taken down in writing and may be used in evidence if I can spell it.

BERT: Anybody can spell it — I T, it!

H. M. (screeching): A most horrible suspicion is beginning to cross my mind . . .

GOBLINS: Ooooo!

BERT: She reminds me of my Auntie Ethel except for the moustache.

P. C. PARKER: But she hasn't got a moustache!

BERT: No, but my Auntie Ethel has.

H. M. (screeching as before): A horrible *horrible* suspicion.

GOBLINS: Oooh!

H. M.: That these humans are *not* children!

BERT: Of course we're not . . . you can't kid us.

P. C. PARKER: Mind you, we used to be children. I was a beautiful child. (Takes out photo.) This is me at the seaside at the age of five. This is my sister Gladys — she's standing on her head —

H. M.: That's no use to me . . .

GOBLINS: Oooooooo!

H. M. (leaping up): Dethrone!

(The GOBLINS disentangle themselves and stand in a shivering apprehensive group, trying to stand behind each other to escape the wrath.)

Never in my entire rain and snow have I seen such disgraceful — (Through megaphone.) — DISGRACEFUL incompetence and stupidity . . .

P. C. PARKER: That's right, you tell them.

H. M.: Shuttup.

BERT: You can't tell the Law to shuttup.

JENNY: Don't speak like that to Her Marshesty.

H. M. (to JENNY): Shuttup . . . where was I?

GOB: Disgraceful . . .

SLURP: Incompetence . . .

TWERP: And er . . .

P. C. PARKER: Loss of memory?

GOBLINS: SHUTTUP.

(They begin to sing the Marshellaise.)

H. M., BERT, JENNY & P. C. PARKER: SHUTTUP.

(The GOBLINS shut up.)

H. M.: It is essential that I have *children* brought to me . . . little, frightened, helpless children who are easy to KICK (Kicks GOB.) and tweak (Tweaks TWERP's ear.) and pull the hair of (pulls SLURP's hair. The GOBLINS snivel and squawk.) and twist the arms of (Twists GOB's arm.) and scream in the ear of (Screams at TWERP.) and shake till their teeth rattle in their heads (Shakes SLURP.).

(The GOBLINS are snivelling heaps.)

I want to hear them crying and see them miserable and terrified. I want to see those tiny faces with big tears rolling down their pale cheeks, once rosy with health, now drained from captivity in the marsh . . . I want to see them REALLY UNHAPPY.

P. C. PARKER: I think I've discovered a fact about this old queen.

BERT: What's that?

P. C. PARKER: I don't think she likes children very much.

H. M.: Rubbish and litter! Of course I do . . . I LOVE children . . . because they're easy to KICK . . . and TWEAK . . .

GOBLINS: No no H. M. not again . . . Ooooooo!

H. M.: . . . and TICKLE!

(The GOBLINS are paralysed with terror.)

P. C. PARKER: Really?

H. M.: Oh yes!

(She tickles GOBLINS. They collapse, helpless. H. M. starts to tickle members of the audience.)

P. C. PARKER (parting the affray): Come along now, Your Marshesty, that'll be enough of that . . .

H. M.: Take your nasty clean hands off me . . . (To the GOBLINS.) You see? These big children are no good . . . If I tweak and kick and punch them, they seem likely to hit me back . . . not to mention me front!

JENNY: What glittering wit, Your Marshesty.

H. M.: Yes . . . perhaps they'll do . . . WHY couldn't you find any little children today?

GOB: There weren't any left in the market.

H. M.: You mean they'd all been sold?

P. C. PARKER: All the nippers in the district are being kept at home because SOMEONE is stealing them away.

H. M.: Kidnipping! Isn't it shocking! Really, what will people do next . . . it just spoils life for us honest people, doesn't it.

GOBLINS: No, er yes . . . er we don't know what to reply.

H. M.: Just agree with me, you idiots . . . RIGHT, these specimens will have to do I suppose . . . I'm going to collect a snack. Get ready for the ORDEAL . . . PREPARE.

(Everyone freezes.)

ANNOUNCER: What ordeal has this wicked Monarch in store for our heroes? Return to this place in twelve minutes for the next amazing adventure in the case of the INCREDIBLE VANISHING.

(Blackout. Dramatic chord — from 'Legend of the Glass Mountain'.)

END OF ACT ONE

ACT TWO

Blackout. Dramatic chord.

ANNOUNCER: Everybody stand by for scenes of mystery, danger, magic and terror . . .

(The lights come on to reveal everyone frozen as at the end of Act One.)

Our friends have made their way into the cavern under the Marsh to rescue Jenny Jones from the spell of the enchanted apple, when suddenly they hear a voice which commands . . .

(Everyone springs to life.)

H. M.: Get ready for the ORDEAL. PREPARE.

(The GOBLINS play the Marshellaise and H. M. sings. They all go off.)

Squelch squelch squelch
Here comes the Queen.
Squelch squelch squelch
I'm really mean.

BERT: I don't believe it . . . unless there's other Marsh Goblins on guard in the tunnels, we can escape before H. M. gets back.

(Sound of children's cries.)

P. C. PARKER (indicating that he means the audience): We must try to rescue all these children who are prisoners in the Marsh . . .

JENNY: Rescue? But this place is beautiful . . . why would anyone want to leave it ever?

P. C. PARKER: I don't think that crying we heard sounded like people who think it's beautiful here.

BERT: Come on, quick, let's run away . . .

P. C. PARKER: At least we'll get out of this cavern . . . come on, Jenny, come with us . . .

JENNY (very drowsy): No . . . No, I want to stay here . . .

P. C. PARKER: She's still under the spell of that enchanted apple . . . Mr Sparky, take her other arm, we'll try to help her along . . . come on, Jenny . . . (She resists.)

JENNY: No . . . no, I want to stay here . . .

P. C. PARKER: *Please* – can't you see how horrible this place is?

JENNY: Sweet music . . . summer sun . . .

(The Marshellaise is heard again.)

P. C. PARKER: Here they come again . . . quick, Mr Sparky . . . we'll conceal ourselves and continue our observation of the suspected persons in accordance with routine police procedure.

BERT: Eh?

P. C. PARKER: We'll hide and watch them. Quick . . .

(They hide.)

BERT: Don't worry, Jenny, we'll be near.

JENNY (nearly asleep): Blue sea shimmer . . . white sands . . .

(H. M. and GOBLINS return. A recording of the Marshellaise is played. H. M. has a large jamjar full of disgusting liquid.)

H. M.: Thank you! THANK YOU!

(The tape judders to a halt.)

There's nothing I like better than a nice glass of bathwater. (Sips.) Ah! . . . newly gushed from the drain, full of soapy scum!

GOB: Grub up, Your Marshesty!

(He hurls a dustbin on casters across the stage.)

H. M.: Ah, meals on wheels! STOOL!

(TWERP goes down on all fours as a stool.)

Now, what's on the menu?

(The lid is lifted and a swarm of flies buzz out. H. M. and the GOBLINS swat at them.)

GOBLINS: Yum yum!

H. M.: Let's see . . . Tea leaves . . . fishbones . . . ah! Delicious . . . potato peelings! Oh, you spoil me! (She munches some.) Plate!

(GOB holds out his hand as a plate.)

MARSHESTY BEGUINE

GOBLINS (sing, accompanied by TWERP on dustbin lids):
Good crunching to your Marshesty,
Gluttony's no sin.
Good crunching to your Marshesty,
Why not begin — the big bin?
Munch munch munch.

H. M.: I hate canned music! Well, get on with it then — bring the children forward!

GOB: Well, get on with it then, bring the children forward!

SLURP: Well, get on with it then, bring the children for — they've gone!

GOB: They've gone!

H. M.: They've gone?

TWERP (bangs on bin): There's one.

H. M.: BEGIN!

(The GOBLINS push JENNY forward.)

GOBLINS: Your Marshesty's VICTIM.

H. M.: It's asleep, wake it up.

(The GOBLINS pinch JENNY awake.)

JENNY: Ow! Where am I?

(The GOBLINS laugh unpleasantly. H. M. bawls the Marshellaise through her megaphone.)

What a horrible place! Please stop that dreadful noise . . .

H. M.: That's not very polite, is it, Gobs?

GOBLINS: No, Your Marshesty . . .

JENNY: Where's the market? Where's P. C. Parker?

H. M.: Where's the longest river in the world?

JENNY: Er . . . I don't know . . . Where is the longest river in the world?

H. M.: In between its banks. .

(The GOBLINS shriek.)

JENNY: Can I have a drink . . . I'm so thirsty.

(The GOBLINS shriek and approach with the apple.)

GOB: Try this!

JENNY: No, I'm thirsty, not hungry.

GOB: But this is juicy.

SLURP: And succulent.

TWERP: And luscious.

(JENNY takes a bite.)

H. M.: And enchanted.

JENNY: Oh!

GOB (grabs the apple from her): Grab!

H. M.: Feeling better?

JENNY: Yes, thank you . . . beautiful! lady.

H. M.: *Right*! Listen very carefully to what I have to say . . . If you can tell me a story to amuse me, THEN you may eat the rest of that apple which will keep you alive for another day and happy to be here . . .

JENNY: Oh . . .

H. M.: BUT — if your story does NOT amuse me, then you will be locked up in the Drain with all the other children and you will eat only boiled cabbage which will keep you alive and unhappy to be here . . . and you will never never never be allowed to return to the Upper World again.

JENNY: But —

TWERP: Not to mention being kicked and tweaked and having your hair pulled.

H. M.: I'm not GOING to mention that.

JENNY: Well, I know a lot of stories . . .

H. M.: In the last eight hundred years I have not heard any story which has amused me. SWING!

JENNY: Oh!

(Two of the GOBLINS form themselves into a swing. The third pushes.)

H. M.: Story time!

TWERP: Is Your Marshesty sitting comfortably?

H. M.: Yes.

TWERP: Then she'll begin.

(Kazoo fanfare: <u>STORYTIME 1</u>.)

JENNY: Well . . . once upon a time —

H. M.: Heard that one. Haven't I?

GOBLINS: Yes, yes . . .

JENNY (racking her brains): Oh . . . em . . . Well, there was once a . . .

H. M.: Heard that one.

JENNY: Oh . . . well, have you heard the one about the . . .

H. M. (swinging dangerously near JENNY): About the what?

JENNY: About the . . .

H. M.: Well finish your sentence. How do you expect me to know what the story's about if you don't finish your sentences?

JENNY: Oh dear, I can't win . . .

H. M.: I've heard that one . . . all those stories were very BORING . . . UNSWING! (The GOBLINS let her fall to the ground.) You have three minutes human time to think of a story that amuses me . . . otherwise into the Drain for ever. Gob follow me . . . I'll go and hit some children while we're waiting.

GOB: And tweak and punch and pinch?

H.M.: Why not . . . ?

TWERP & SLURP: Can we come too?

H. M.: NO. Watch this human. See it doesn't fall asleep or run away. Follow!

(The Marshellaise. H. M. sweeps off, pinching a few of the audience as she goes. JENNY is left crying beside the steps. TWERP and SLURP start raking in the dustbin for food. Slurping and crunching noises are heard. P. C. PARKER and BERT tiptoe out of hiding.)

P. C. PARKER: There's only one thing to do, Mr Sparky.

BERT: Right! (He sets off at a run.)

P. C. PARKER: No! (Catches him.) We must change places with the goblins.

BERT: What?

P. C. PARKER: Ready? You grab that one, I'll get that one . . .

BERT: Right!

P. C. PARKER: And remember, they become helpless when tickled.

BERT: Don't we all!

(They creep up on the GOBLINS who are still snuffling and crunching in the dustbin, exchanging tasty fishbones and the like.)

BERT & P. C. PARKER: Tickle! Tickle!

(The GOBLINS are helpless. BERT and P. C. PARKER pounce on them and grab their boiler suits off them.)

ANNOUNCER (against a background of heroic music: the overture to 'Zampa'): See our intrepid heroes carry out their daring plan! Hooray! Will their disguise be unmasked by the keen eyes of the wicked Monarch! Will Jenny Jones recover from the spell which enchants her?

(The GOBLINS escape shivering and squawking. BERT and P. C. PARKER are now dressed in boiler suits.)

GOBLINS: We're not allowed to appear naked before Her Marshesty.

(JENNY has watched in amazement.)

JENNY: P. C. Parker, Mr Sparky . . .

P. C. PARKER: You remember who we are?

BERT: That's nice . . .

P. C. PARKER: Don't worry, we'll think of a good story for you to tell
. . . I'm always a riot at concerts.

BERT: And if he can't think of one, I've got a fund of lively tales.

JENNY: I wouldn't mind staying here . . . it's quite nice.

P. C. PARKER: But not beautiful.

JENNY: Not as beautiful as I thought at first . . .

BERT (finding the GOBLINS' hats): We'd better put these on.

(They put them on top of their own hats.)

P. C. PARKER: And their glasses — they're in the pockets.

(The Marshellaise begins again.)

Right, here they come — get the glasses on . . .

BERT: Look at that Marsh Monarch arriving in a royal litter!

(Terrible clattering and shrieking. H. M. arrives in her sedan-chair
pulled by GOB and followed by a large Goblin, BULK. The sedan-
chair rattles and lurches on to the cavern floor. H. M. is blowing
bubbles.)

H. M.: STOP! Slurp! Twerp!

(P. C. PARKER and BERT lurk.)

GOB: Slurp! Twerp! Come here.

P. C. PARKER: I think she means us.

BERT: I think I want to go home.

H. M.: What's the matter with you — why are you wearing your Upper
World eyelids?

BERT & P. C. PARKER (imitating the GOBLINS as best they can):
. . . For fun . . .

H. M.: You've got a funny idea of fun . . . BULK!

BERT: BLIMEY!

BULK: Your Marshesty.

H. M.: Collect that human and stand it over there — it's going to tell a
story . . .

(BULK heads for JENNY.)

P. C. PARKER: That's a big one.

BERT: How many of them do you think there are? Might be an army of
them — he might be an economy size.

P. C. PARKER: We've got to be brave.

BERT: Not likely.

H. M.: Begin.

(Kazoo fanfare: <u>STORYTIME 2</u>.)

Twerp! Slurp! Didn't hear *you.*

(They haven't got kazoos. They imitate a fanfare.)

Pathetic! Begin!

JENNY: Well . . . (Clearing her throat.) Once there was a —

H. M.: I've heard that one.

P. C. PARKER: You can't have heard this one . . .

BERT: It doesn't exist yet.

GOB: She said that without moving her lips.

H. M.: If the story doesn't exist yet then you can't know what it is, so you'd better go to the Drain at once.

BERT: But this is a brand new story . . .

P. C. PARKER: Specially for Your Marshesty.

GOB: She's got a very varied voice, hasn't she?

BULK: Yes.

BERT: BLIMEY!

GOB (beadily to BERT and P. C. PARKER): Hasn't she?

P. C. PARKER BERT	(simultaneously):	Yes. No.
P. C. PARKER BERT	(simultaneously):	No. Yes.

H. M.: SHUTTUP.

BULK (hitting them on their hats with his fists): Bonk!

H. M.: All right, begin.

JENNY: Cinderella was unhappy because —

P. C. PARKER & BERT: We've heard that one.

H. M.: Shuttup.

BULK: Bonk!

(BULK thuds them again.)

P. C. PARKER & BERT: Ow!

JENNY: Because her goldfish had a cold and it was rice pudding again for lunch . . .

H. M. (shuddering): Ugh, well it's a disgusting tale so far.

JENNY: And then . . . all of a sudden . . .

P. C. PARKER: She threw the rice pudden . . .

BERT: And the goldfish fell out on the floor . . .

BOTH: Boom boom.

BULK (thudding them again): Bonk!

BERT & P. C. PARKER: OW!

JENNY (struggling on): When all of a sudden — help me, P. C. Parker . . .

P. C. PARKER: She cried, as the runaway lorry thundered down the hill towards the helpless goldfish lying in the middle of the road. Police Constable Jack Parker, a handsome, intelligent and zealous young officer, leapt from the doorway of the Co-op grocers and . . .

BERT: Fell flat on his face on the pavement.

JENNY: His bootlaces mysteriously tied together by an unseen hand.

P. C. PARKER: With one bound he was free and ran with lithe athletic strides towards the gasping goldfish.

BERT: But he was too late!

P. C. PARKER: No he wasn't.

BERT: Yes he was . . . Henry from the fish barrow had swooped with predatory skill and added the goldfish to the other fish.

JENNY: Yes, he took it back to his plaice.

EVERBYODY: Ugh!

JENNY: Where the Ball was just about to begin . . .

P. C. PARKER: May I have the pleasure of this dance, Prince Charming enquired.

BERT: Clear off, said Jack the Giant Killer, before I hit you with my Beanstalk.

JENNY: What big eyes you have, cried Goldilocks as she . . .

P. C. PARKER: Flung the potato from her with a shudder.

BERT: A real chip off the old block, said Fred the hot pie man nostalgically . . . this raspberry jelly reminds me of . . .

JENNY: My fairy godmother . . . at last you're here — I have left my coach with six white horses outside the palace . . .

P. C. PARKER: Where it collected a parking ticket from Miss Lulu Maguire, Champion Meter Maid of 1975 . . .

BERT & P. C. PARKER (rushing round her in a tight circle): Pick a ticket, flick it, stick it.

H. M.: STOP! STOP! . . . I have reached a royal decision about this story.

JENNY: Yes?

H. M.: We are *not* amused. To the Drain!

(P. C. PARKER and BERT rush forward.)

P. C. PARKER: I say, I say, I say, how do you know if an elephant's been in your fridge?

BERT: I don't know . . . how do you know if an elephant's been in you fridge?

P. C. PARKER: By the footprints in the butter!

BOTH: BOOBOOM!

(H. M. and GOBLINS are baffled.)

P. C. PARKER: Doesn't that amuse you?

H. M.: I don't know . . . what was it about?

BERT: What was it about?

H. M.: Yes, what was it about? I'm getting a horrible, *horrible* suspicion . . .

GOB & BULK: Oooo.

H. M.: That you two Goblins have been corrupted by your visits to the Upper World . . .

JENNY: I thought it was an amusing story . . .

BERT: Thank you, Jenny.

P. C. PARKER: Er, we don't know what your name is.

H. M.: How do you know if a Nellifant's been in your fridge?

GOB: By the footprints in the butter . . . Booboom!

H. M.: It's pathetic. To the Dra . . . What's a Nellifant?

P. C. PARKER: An elephant?

BERT: Everybody knows what an elephant is.

H. M.: I don't.

GOBLINS: We don't.

H. M.: That's three of us for a start.

P. C. PARKER: Well, it's kind of a —

BERT: It's very big —

P. C. PARKER: With a sort of —

JENNY: Very grey . . .

P. C. PARKER: We'll show you.

(They've been waving their hands about . . . and begin to form themselves into an elephant — JENNY at the front as the trunk with her arms stretched forward, BERT as the ears with the two hats and P. C. PARKER as the back end with one arm as the tail. They all trumpet and walk about.)

(To the others): Walk to the tunnel then start running.

(They head for the tunnel.)

H. M.: All right, we get the idea. *Come back!* We get the idea.

(They have to come back.)

So there's been one of those nellifants in your fridge . . . What's 'your fridge'?

BERT: Well, it just stands there and hums.

P. C. PARKER: Like those Goblins.

GOB: Twerp, Slurp.

BULK: What's the matter with you?

P. C. PARKER: Imitation of a fridge . . . HUMMMMMMMMMM.

(BERT goes up to P. C. PARKER and, by moving his arm, 'opens the door'.)

BERT: There you are, ice cubes, butter, streaky bacon, fish fingers.

H. M.: I didn't know fish had fingers.

BERT: Neither did I.

P. C. PARKER: Right, so there you have it . . . you know by the footprints in the butter . . .

BERT: If an elephant's been in your fridge.

BULK: Booboom!

H. M.: In all my years in the Marsh by mind has never been so boggled. (Mutters.) How do you know if an elephant's been in your fridge? By the footprints in the butta booboom.

(Out loud): What exactly is butta?

P. C. PARKER: It's manufactured with milk.

BERT: Which comes from a cow.

H. M.: COW?

(BERT and P. C. PARKER do an imitation of a cow . . . using one hand for udder, two arms for the horn.)

H. M.: I thought that was a nellifant.

BERT & P. C. PARKER: No, *this* is an elephant.

(They spring into their imitation of an elephant.)

P. C. PARKER: Other tunnel!

H. M.: STOP ! STOP! STOP! All right, I get the idea — sort of. Now this butta is for drinking right?

P. C. PARKER: Wrong.

BERT: It's for spreading on bread.

JENNY: You've heard of bread?

H. M (shuddering): Yes. DISGUSTING HORRIBLE MUCK . . .

GOBLINS: UGH!

H. M.: I like good wholesome food — like well seeped potato peelings . . .

GOBLINS: Mmmmm!

H. M.: And really old sopping tea leaves . . . with just a touch of mildewed turnip.

JENNY: Ugh! That's horrible.

H. M.: You mean *you* don't like it, that's not the same thing.

BERT: But you don't like bread and butter.

H. M.: That's horrible.

P. C. PARKER: You mean you don't like it, that's not the same thing.

H. M.: Oh yes it is . . . If *I* don't like something, it's horrible, if *you* don't like something it means that you're silly . . . that's what being a Monarch is all about —

GOBLINS & H. M.: See!

H. M.: Take that human and lock it in the Drain.

JENNY: Oh no . . .

P. C. PARKER & BERT: Right on, Your Marshesty, we'll do it . . .

H. M.: No, you won't . . . BULK, take the human to the deepest and darkest part of the Drain.

BULK: Very good, Your Marshesty . . . (Grabs JENNY.)

JENNY (crying): Oh . . .

(BULK and JENNY disappear into the tunnel.)

H. M.: I'm absolutely drained with all this difficult conversation. I'm going to have a nap. BED!

BERT & P. C. PARKER: Right.

(They set off in the direction of the tunnels.)

GOB: Twerp, Slurp, didn't you hear what H. M. said?

BERT: Yes, she's going to bed.

P. C. PARKER: So we'll leave her to it.

GOB: What's the matter with you two today? You know perfectly well that we make the bed and She lies on it.

P. C. PARKER & BERT (baffled): We make the bed and she lies on it!

H. M.: You look as if you'd never made a bed before.

BERT: Well, we haven't!

P. C. PARKER: We haven't forgotten.

H. M.: Right! Get on with it then! BED!

GOB: Hup!

P. C. PARKER & BERT: Hup!

(GOB throws himself to the ground face down. BERT and P. C. PARKER follow suit one on either side of GOB.)

H. M. (yawning): We're in for a rough night!

(She lies on top of them.)

LULLABY!

LULLABY FOR H. M.

GOB (sings, accompanied by off-stage voices);	Slurp to sleep Your Marshesty, Drains are up above . . .
BERT & P. C. PARKER:	Wah wah.
GOB:	We hope your dreams are full of filth And slime and scum and fluff . . .
BERT & P. C. PARKER:	Wah wah wah.
GOB:	May each unconscious moment Be entirely rubbish filled . . .
BERT & P. C. PARKER:	Wah wah wah.
GOB:	And from the sewer of your mind No precious thought be spilled . . .
ALL:	Till you awaken — waa waah.
BERT & P. C. PARKER:	Slurp to sleep Your Marshesty . . . (H. M. snores.) Glad to hear you snored . . . (H. M. snores.) Wah wah.
BERT:	Want to know what's wrong with me? Well, I am bed and bored . . .

VOICES (off-stage):	Ugh!
P. C. PARKER:	Slurp to sleep Your Marshesty,
	This is your mattress
	Whose public duty is to take
	Your name and your address . . .
ALL:	Because we hate you — a-aah! (Everybody snores.)

(H. M. begins to snore disgustingly, as does GOB. BERT and P. C. PARKER nod off.)

P. C. PARKER: Bert! Bert!

(He blows his whistle. BERT wakes with a start.)

BERT: Rosy bananas! You're a really clever bloke, aren't you . . . look at us trapped underneath this smelly old marshmallow . . . and Jenny Jones locked up in the Drain for ever. Great!

P. C. PARKER: Don't panic.

BERT: Who's panicking?

P. C. PARKER: I'll think of something.

BERT: Now I'm panicking!

(H. M. turns in her sleep. Her hand falls over BERT's or P. C. PARKER's face.)

BERT or P. C. PARKER: UGH! (Throws hand off.)

P. C. PARKER (of GOB's bad breath): His best friend should tell him.

BERT: Shouldn't think he's got one!

P. C. PARKER: Wait a minute . . . do you see what I see?

BERT: What?

P. C. PARKER: Look what's coming through the tunnel . . .

(Snivelling and slurping noises are heard. TWERP and SLURP trail down the tunnels.)

SLURP: She'll tweak our ears.

TWERP: Shuttup!

SLURP: And pull our hair.

TWERP: Oooooooo!

P. C. PARKER: And kick your shins.

TWERP & SLURP: Oooooo!

BERT: And twist your nasty little twiggy arms.

TWERP & SLURP: Oooooo — hey!

SLURP: Look at that!

TWERP: There's somebody sleeping as our bed!

BERT: You've dribbled a bibful baby.

P. C. PARKER: Would you like us to assist you out of your predicament?

SLURP: No thanks, but can you get us out of this mess.

P. C. PARKER: Right . . . help us out of this bed and we'll give you back your clothes, then you take our places and Her Marshesty will never know you've been away.

(H. M. suddenly sits up and shrieks. TWERP and SLURP help her to stand.)

H. M. (sings to the tune of 'Aquarius'): This is the downing of the garbage of aquariums . . .

P. C. PARKER: That's a bit of luck, Bert!

BERT: She's sleepwalking!

P. C. PARKER: Quick!

(H. M. 'sleepwalks' around the stage. Meanwhile TWERP and SLURP help BERT and P. C. PARKER out of their boilersuits, put them on, and lie down in their places. H. M. finishes her circle and is helped onto the bed by BERT and P. C. PARKER.)

ANNOUNCER (with chords from 'Zampa' in the background): What an amazing stroke of good fortune! The dreams of the evil Queen are nightly haunted by visions of – (H. M. does 'nellifant' impersonation.) – who can tell? Will our heroes escape from the loathly bed of the wicked Monarch? Can they change clothes before Her Marshesty awakens? Can they make good their escape? Can they rescue Jenny Jones?

BERT & P. C. PARKER: Would you mind being quiet?

ANNOUNCER: Sorry!

> LULLABY FOR H. M. (Reprise)

BERT & P. C. PARKER (sing):
> Slurp to sleep Your Marshesty,
> Now it's very clear . . .
> Wah wah . . .
> That Bert and P. C. Parker
> Are skipping out of here . . .

(They skip out down the aisle.)

H. M.: MORNING!

(She springs up and the GOBLINS sing.)

MARSHESTY GREETING

GOBLINS (singing):
> Bad morning to Your Marshesty,
> My word you do look well.
> Bad morning to Your Marshesty,
> How horrible you smell.

H. M.: Thank you . . . (She goes into the cavern and looks in the food bucket.) Slurp, Twerp, tell me about the nellifant again.

GOB: Twerp, Slurp . . . tell Her Marshesty about the nellifant again.

TWERP: About the . . .

SLURP: Nellifant?

H. M. (getting beady): Have you got cloth ears? Do you want them *tweaked*?

TWERP & SLURP: Noooooo.

H. M.: Come along . . . (She does an imitation as best she can of the trumpeting and mooing and humming.) Nellifant!

TWERP & SLURP (watch fascinated): Oooooo!

H. M.: Cow! (She does an imitation of a cow.)

TWERP & SLURP: Ooh!

H. M.: Well?

TWERP & SLURP (giggle): It's very silly, Your Marshesty.

GOB: You invented it, you should know.

TWERP: Us?

SLURP: Us?

H. M.: Yes.

GOB: You.

TWERP & SLURP: Ooooooo.

H.M.: I have a horrible *horrible* suspicion.

GOBLINS: OOOOOOO!

H. M.: That those goblins were IMPOSTORS.

GOBLINS: Oooo.

H. M.: Worse than that, I think they were HUMANS!

GOBLINS: Oooooo.

H. M. (Sniffing): Yes . . . there's a distinct smell of humans in the atmosphere . . . FOLLOW!

(They collide as they rush for the tunnel – towards one aisle.)

Stop! Go! Not that way, you fools . . . take the express drain. Wait for me!

(They rush into the other aisle with the sedan-chair. JENNY, P. C. PARKER and BERT return down the first aisle.)

P. C. PARKER: Hurry, Jenny, please . . .

JENNY: But I must have just one more taste of that beautiful apple . . . you must try one too . . .

P. C. PARKER: Still enchanted.

BERT: What are we going to do? You heard what that big Bulk said just before we hit him on the head.

P. C. PARKER: Yes – don't hit me on the head! Unless she can eat food from the Upper World she won't want to return with us.

BERT: Haven't we got any food with us?

P. C. PARKER (searching his pockets): Wait a minute . . . I think I've got some. Ah, yes . . . (Pulls out a tube of Smarties.) Here we are . . . Oh, it's empty!

JENNY (sings 'I will sing a rainbow'): Red and yellow and orange and green . . .

BERT: That's it . . . orange, I've got an orange in me pocket . . . I picked one up from the ground . . .

(He puts his hands in his pockets and takes an orange from each. Both have faces on them – one smiling, one miserable.)

P. C. PARKER: You've got two oranges.

BERT: Yes . . . and one of them is enchanted . . . and I can't remember which one.

JENNY: You feel happy and clever and good . . .

P. C. PARKER: Wait a minute now. I'm going to eat a bit of this orange . . . if it's enchanted you'll soon know, and you can quickly give me – and Jenny too, a piece of the other orange. Right?

BERT: Right.

P. C. PARKER: Here goes . . . (He eats bit of the orange.)

BERT: Well?

P. C. PARKER (going mad): Fantastic . . . what a beautiful place, I want to stay here forever . . . wheeeee!

(BERT looks horrified. P. C. PARKER stops larking about and becomes official.)

It's all right, Mr Sparky, this is the genuine Jaffa.

BERT: What a fright . . . here you are, Jenny.

JENNY: Ugh, no it looks horrible and smells disgusting.

P. C. PARKER: You must . . .

JENNY: No.

P. C. PARKER: It's full of . . . cinders and hooverdust. It's lovely.

JENNY: NO.

BERT (pointing): Look at that extraordinary bluebird on the roof.

JENNY (looking up): Oh, where?

P. C. PARKER: Right . . . (Squeezes orange against JENNY's mouth.)

BERT: That's it.

JENNY: Ugh . . .

P. C. PARKER: Sorry, Jenny . . .

JENNY: Ugh . . . what a . . . what a horrible place, I don't want to stay here, it's very nasty and frightening.

P. C. PARKER: And is that the verdict of us all?

ALL THREE: YES!

P. C. PARKER: Right, let's get out of here.

(They head for the upstage exit.)

H. M. (appearing at upstage exit): Not so fast, humans . . . aren't you going to say goodbye?

THREE: Goodbye. (They head for the first aisle.)

H. M.: BULK!

(BULK appears bulkily from the first aisle.)

BERT: Oh Gor blimey.

P. C. PARKER: This way!

H. M.: Gob!

(GOB appears menacingly from the second aisle.)

H. M.: It's no good thinking you can escape . . . as long as the human with the yellow stripe on its head wants to stay here . . .

JENNY: But I don't.

P. C. PARKER: Bad luck, H. M. — we found some Upper World food, so she's no longer enchanted.

H. M. (screeching): WHAT!!

THREE: Goodbye!

H. M. (sweetly): All right, you've been very clever . . . you can go . . .
BUT if you —

JENNY: Me?

H. M. (to JENNY): Just you — look back before you reach the tunnel,
then you will have to stay here forever . . . with no chance of escape.

P. C. PARKER: Well, thank you . . .

BERT: That's dead easy — it's only a few yards . . .

JENNY: Quick!

H. M. (into her megaphone): PLAN A.

TWERP (off-stage): Plan A, Your Marshesty!

(There is a dull clang. The THREE find that their feet are like lead,
and a fierce current of air prevents them from moving fast.)

BERT: What's happening?

JENNY: I can't walk.

P. C. PARKER: What's she done to us?

H. M.: The door of the Great Sewer has been opened and released the air
pressure in the tunnels . . . soon the water will follow and sweep you
all away.

P. C. PARKER: And sweep you away too . . .

H. M.: No thanks, I can swim, I've put on my water-wings. Look.

(JENNY is about to turn round.)

BERT & P. C. PARKER: DON't look round . . .

H. M.: Quite right, she might see that big hungry rat about to bite her
ankle . . .

JENNY: Aaagh!

BERT & P. C. PARKER: Don't look round!

(They are nearly out of the cavern.)

H. M. (getting desperate): Quick! Run back . . . Here comes the water!

THREE: We won't look back.

H. M. (screeching): PLAN B!

TWERP (off-stage): Plan B, Your Marshesty!

(Another dull clang. The air current stops.)

P. C. PARKER: Run!

(They are face to face with themselves.)

THREE: Aaaagh!

> (TWERP and SLURP have come on and are holding a large mirror in front of the three. They back into the cavern. H. M. arranges herself behind them so that they can see her reflected in the mirror.)

H. M. (shrieking triumphantly): You looked back!

> (GOBLINS shout with glee.)

BERT & P. C. PARKER: That's not fair!

JENNY: I haven't looked back!

H. M.: Yes you have!

P. C. PARKER: Shut your eyes.

H. M. & GOBLINS: YOU LOOKED BACK!

JENNY: No, I didn't!

H. M. & GOBLINS: Yes you did!

JENNY (turning back): NO! I didn't! . . .

> (Kazoo chord.)

H. M. (beadily): NOW you have!

JENNY: Oh!

BERT & P. C. PARKER: Oh, no!

H. M.: Oh yes, and now you'll have to stay in the Drain with no enchanted apples to eat, in the damp darkness . . . for *ever.* Bulk! To the Drain!

> (BULK takes JENNY away down the first aisle. The other GOBLINS take the mirror and scuttle back.)

P. C. PARKER: I'll contact the police station . . . (To his radio.) . . . send for reinforcements . . . Hello, Headquarters . . . hello, Headquarters, this is P. C. 240 . . . do you read me . . . over . . .

> (The radio plays pop music. He turns it off.)

BERT: Fat lot of good that is.

P. C. PARKER: I should never have changed the radio for my tranny . . .

BERT: Oi . . . Your Marshyness, we'll tell you a story to make you laugh . . . this old age pensioner goes in the Post Office . . .

P. C. PARKER: Have you heard the one about the —

H. M.: Stop! Stop! What was that delicious noise?

BERT: That was us . . .

P. C. PARKER: . . . saying 'have you heard the one about the . . . '

H. M.: No . . . it was a noise . . . it was beautiful . . .

GOB: Was it us going . . . (Kazoo chord.)

H. M.: NO! NO! it was a noise . . . that was in that magic box . . . (Points at the radio.)

BERT: That's not a magic box, that's only a – OW!

(P. C. PARKER has kicked his shin.)

P. C. PARKER: This magic box?

H. M.: I want to hear the noise again.

P. C. PARKER: Very well!

(P. C. PARKER hands it over.)

BERT: What are you doing?

P. C. PARKER: Ssh!

H. M. (turning the radio and shaking it): It won't make a noise for me.

P. C. PARKER: Allow me! Mr Sparky?

BERT: Yes?

P. C. PARKER: Standby to operate magic box.

BERT: Standing by – absolute silence please.

H. M.: SILENCE!

BERT: Silence!

H. M.: SORRY!

P. C. PARKER: Transistors.

BERT: Check!

P. C. PARKER: Batteries.

BERT: Check!

P. C. PARKER: Wavelengths.

BERT: Check!

P. C. PARKER: Chrysanthemums.

BERT: Cheek!

P. C. PARKER: Standby to operate magic box.

BERT: Radio 4 – 3 – 2 – 1.

P. C. PARKER: Pip! We have switch on!

(He switches on the radio. It plays pop music. P. C. PARKER tunes it through a variety of programmes, ending with music to which they all dance.)

H. M. & GOBLINS: Ooooo! (They listen, rapt.)

(P. C. PARKER switches the radio off abruptly.)

P. C. PARKER: Goodbye, then — we're off — come on, Mr Sparky.

BERT: But —

P. C. PARKER: Come along, Mr Sparky . . . we're going now.

H. M.: Wait . . . don't go — I want to hear the noise again.

P. C. PARKER: Don't you want to hear a story to amuse you — Once upon a time . . .

H. M.: No, I don't want to hear a story . . . I want to . . . HEAR THAT NOISE.

BERT: I want I want never gets.

H. M.: Let me hear the magic again.

P. C. PARKER: What do you say?

H. M. (as if the word was obscene): Please!

GOBLINS (collapse in a heap): Ooooooh!

P. C. PARKER: Well, I don't know . . . I think we'd better go. What do you think, Mr Sparky?

BERT: Yes, well, I don't know either.

P. C. PARKER: I think we'd better go, don't you?

BERT: No — yes — I think we'd better go.

H. M.: You can ask for anything in the underworld — Goblins for Slaves!

GOBLINS: Ooooo!

P. C. PARKER: No thanks.

H. M.: Gold . . . you humans like gold . . . we find a lot of gold swirling round here . . .

P. C. PARKER: No thanks.

BERT: Not likely.

H. M.: Anything . . . I'll give you *anything* . . .

P. C. PARKER: Let Jenny Jones go free.

H. M.: What's a jeni-jones?

P. C. PARKER: The young lady with the yellow line round her head.

H. M.: NO!

P. C. PARKER: All right, we're off.

H. M.: No, stop, very well, she can go!

P. C. PARKER & BERT: Hooray!

P. C. PARKER: AND you must return all the children you've stolen!

H. M. & GOBLINS: NO!

(P. C. PARKER plays the radio and switches it off.)

H. M.: I don't care . . . I'd rather have a Drainful of unhappy children.

P. C. PARKER: I must warn you that since you have heard the magic you will be unable to look at all these children imprisoned here without seeing terrible red spots before the eyes.

(The auditorium lights go on.)

ANNOUNCER: All the children imprisoned in the Drain look inside their copies of The Daily Marsh which luckily they have with them. In the centre is a red spot. They show the Red Spots to the wicked Monarch.

H. M.: Red spots? Rubbish . . . I'm looking very closely at those miserable children and I can't see any . . .

(Sees the red spots held up by the audience.)

Aaaaaargh . . . Yes, I can . . . horrible red spots!

GOBLINS: We see them too . . . OOOOO!

BERT: So do I . . . Ugh!

P. C. PARKER: Well?

H. M.: I give in, I give in. They can return to the Upper World . . .

P. C. PARKER: AND you promise you'll never steal any more children.

H. M. (grudgingly): All right.

P. C. PARKER: Good!

H. M.: Not till next week.

P. C. PARKER: Beware of the red spots before the eyes.

H. M. (looking at audience): Ugh, there they are again! . . . Very well . . . no more children stealing!

P. C. PARKER: All right, kids. You can put your spots away.

(The auditorium lights go out. JENNY runs down the aisle towards P. C. PARKER.)

Jenny! You're free to go.

JENNY: But what about all the children locked up in the Drain?

BERT: Shut up and keep walking before Her Marshyness changes her mind!

JENNY: If she's got one!

(BERT and JENNY go off.)

GOBLINS: Ooooooooooh.

H. M.: SHUT UP! Hand over the magic box.

P. C. PARKER: First I will instruct you in how to operate the magic box. Take the box in the right hand. Poise the royal index finger over the switch, then repeat the magic formula after me: YAMA.

H. M.: YAMA

P. C. PARKER: REELY

H. M.: REELY

P. C. PARKER: SEELY

H. M.: SEELY

P. C. PARKER: IDJIT

H. M.: IDJIT

P. C. PARKER: And now switch on.

H. M.: YAMA REELY SEELY IDJIT!

(H. M. turns the radio on. It plays a Cliff Richard song.)

OOO! I can make the magic box speak!

(H. M. parades around repeating the formula and switching the radio on and off, as P. C. PARKER leaves. The lights go down on the cavern and come up on the street. JENNY and BERT emerge through the door of the pillar-box into the street, as H. M. and the GOBLINS go off into the recesses of the Drains.)

JENNY: Isn't it great to breathe fresh air again . . .

BERT: Yes . . . (Takes breath.) I wouldn't exactly call it fresh . . . Still it's better than nothing I suppose . . .

JENNY: Where's P. C. Parker?

BERT: Looks like he's lost in the post . . .

(P. C. PARKER emerges from the pillar-box.)

P. C. PARKER: 'Evening, all!

JENNY (hugs him): *Thank* you, P. C. Parker.

P. C. PARKER: All in the line of duty, Miss. All the children are ready to go home . . .

JENNY: What's happened to Her Marshesty?

P. C. PARKER: Listen . . .

(From inside the pillar-box we hear the distant radio and shrieks and Ooooo's.)

Mind you, I don't know what she'll do when the batteries run out . . .

JENNY: Oo! Quick, shut the door . . .

BERT (getting his barrow): And clear off quick . . .

P. C. PARKER: Right, everybody . . . let's go home – mind how you go!

ANNOUNCER: All children are now free to return to their homes . . . So ends one of the most amazing adventures of our time . . . The INCREDIBLE VANISHING . . .

<u>MARKET SONG</u> (Reprise)
JENNY, BERT & P. C. PARKER (sing):
    . . . Good old days three months ago,
    When there wasn't any nasty slippy slidy snow,
    Children everywhere,
    And the noises of the market in the air.
    Oooooooooooooo!
GOBLINS & H. M.:
    Yama reely seely idjit!
EVERYBODY:
    And the jets from all parts of the world in the sky,
    And the kids from the school let out to play,
    And the people out shopping and spending their pay,
    And the beautiful beautiful traffic
    A roaring and a hooting and a parking all day.

(The song speeds up as they exit waving good-bye.)

THE END

Notes on performing
THE INCREDIBLE VANISHING!!!!

Stage

THE INCREDIBLE VANISHING!!!! was written to be performed in the
space of the Young Vic Theatre, where, as well as a raised end-stage,
there is a large thrust-stage with the audience on three sides. To produce
the play in a proscenium setting may present problems; however, the
main requirement is to have two distinct areas for the upper and under-
worlds — defined by lighting or rostra. For the underworld it is essential
to have two exits into the audience and one upstage. The reason for this
is that the audience of children become the prisoners of the Marsh Queen
as described in the play, and contact with the audience is very important
in the underworld (e.g. the 'rat' pursued by P. C. Parker among the feet
of the audience, and the tickling of the children by H. M.).

The street area needs only the pillar-box, which has to be slightly
larger than real size for the entrance and exits through the door. It is best
if the tunnel underneath the box is able to be seen — at the Young Vic
we had the pillar-box on the upper stage with a ladder leading down into
the pit below and the rostrum fronted by gauze so that the ladder could
be revealed when Jenny Jones made her descent into the underworld.

In the case of a school hall, it should be possible to use the raised stage
as the street and to clear a floor area in front of that for the underworld.
The seating could be arranged round this arena area to leave the two
aisles described above.

Props

Bert Sparky's fruit barrow should present no problems, if, like us, you
have a generous and helpful salad dealer in a nearby market. It's a
traditional, flat, market barrow which also serves as a stall. We also had
generous help from the British Apple and Pear Development Council,
who gave us the apples. The Goblins' barrow should look like a barrow
from 'Beano' or 'Dandy' — made from a beer-crate with a toy pram
wheel at the front, and handles made from scrap wood.

Her Marshesty's sedan-chair can be as elaborate or simple as you like
— our designer, John MacFarlane, created a litter based on my idea of a
metal dustbin with the front cut out to make the chair, and put on
handles for carrying. He added the most beautiful superstructure like a
web of metal, surmounted by a gloomy bunch of feathers.

The mirror should be circular; ours was six feet in radius and was
simply a piece of hardboard hinged in the middle and covered with a
superior type of tin foil.

Music and Sound Effects

The music for the play is all pastiche; the accompaniments are indicated in the score. If anyone is puzzled by the word kazoo, it's the submarine-shaped instrument which, when hummed into, produces the effect of a comb and paper being played. We recorded a massed kazoo version of The Marshellaise and of the whistled Theme of the Marshgoblins. Their use is indicated in the text.

We also recorded ourselves the effect of children crying.

Effects of wind howling and water rushing can be bought on commercial sound effects disc, but if you have time to experiment, you can probably record them yourselves.

The radio announcer's voice should be heard over a public address system — he has to speak live, because he has to time his remarks with the other actors. Ideally, he should be able to see the action. He can be played by the actor playing Bulk.

I've indicated in the text the music we used for dramatic effects (e.g. Glass Mountain, Zampa overture) but I'm sure there are others just as dramatic! The same applies to the radio pop music. The one you must have is The Skaters' Waltz because of the plot. The composition of the radio excerpt in Act Two when P. C. Parker is charming Her Marshesty can be as long a sequence as you like . . . we had various kinds of music . . . Victor Sylvester, Rolling Stones, a talk, the signature tune of the Archers (at which the P. C. loyally stood to attention and saluted) and so on, so that there was plenty of opportunity for dances of various kinds (Bert and H. M. in a luscious tango) as the radio was tuned along its wavelength.

Characters

The queen of the Marsh Kingdom should be played by an actor, wearing the most outrageously glamorous gown available . . . but remember 'she' has very pointed ears, as have her subjects.

The Goblins can look just as you like to imagine them . . . our designer created heads for them on a balaclava-helmet basis with one horn on top of their heads, as if they were distant relatives of the unicorn. When Twerp and Slurp had their boiler suits taken off they had bright red 'skins' underneath, covered in horrible boils (half ping-pong balls).

The only character not so far mentioned is Lulu Maguire, who stays in the upperworld searching for her lost book, presumably. She is best played as an Australian — no grudge against Australians, it just sounds marvellous.

Before and After

When we did the play a second time in December 1973, I added a sequence of music at the beginning of the play — a group of buskers entertain the audience with whatever they can play. The company was so talented that we were able to have trumpet, clarinet, electric organ, guitar and drums, tap dancing and musical spoons. Lulu Maguire joined in this sequence and gave a spirited rendering of Waltzing Matilda, helped in the chorus by the audience. It makes a very good start to the play, because after the warm-up, the buskers can enquire of Lulu why the street is deserted, and she replies:

LULU: Haven't you heard the news?

BUSKER: No.

ANNOUNCER: Here is the news.

LULU: Listen!

(ANNOUNCER makes opening announcement of play; as BERT shouts and pop music starts, BUSKERS and LULU rush off screaming.)

But it's entirely to taste, this alternative opening. If you were doing a school production, the bolder members of the orchestra might find it fun to be buskers.

We also added community singing at the end of the play. Since, second time around, it was the Christmas season, we did a version of Twelve Days of Christmas which had new words to it, the twelfth day item being left to the choice of the audience. It was extraordinary how often they chose 'Nellifants'.

One of the very happy consequences of performing the play was the amount of mail from children who'd seen the show. The actors were deluged with delightful — and well observed — drawings and paintings of the characters they played and letters giving remarks and criticisms. For example, one girl wrote to H. M.: 'I'm glad you live in the underworld, it's the best place for you'. A boy wrote 'Dear H. M., I really dig your tasty outfit'. And one of the actors had a letter saying that he was a very good actor and that perhaps one day he'd be as good as Richard Chamberlain!

Music for the Play

MARKET SONG

BERT

A. TEMPO

I wish it was three months ago, when there wasn't any nasty slippy slidey snow.
[speaks] [sings]

BERT

children everywhere and the noises of the market in the air. there was
[speaks]

P.C.

henry and his fishbarrow standing over there ah yes the memory lingers on (sniff)

BERT   P.C.

fine fat haddock, juicy kippers, new caught herring they're good for the nippers there was

JENNY   BERT+P.C.

bill the rag and bone man, and fred the hot-pie stall and violet puke the flower seller

JENNY   3   3   3   BERT+P.C.

sweetest of them all daffodils marigolds sixpence a bunch back in five minutes i've

TUTTI

gone for me lunch in the good old days three months ago

VOICE I

RAG A BONES

when there wasn't any nasty slippy slidey snow

VOICE II

any old iron   juicy hot pies fresh from the oven

VOICE III

lovely old socks , a penny a dozen

children everywhere and the noises of the market in the air oooh

VOICE IV

shoes to mend

THEME OF THE MARSHGOBLINS

IN FREE TIME.
WHISTLED.

GOB: DUST FROM THE DEAD MOON GLITTER FROM AN EVIL STAR LIGHT TO LEAD TRAVELLERS ASTRAY

TO THE KINGDOM WHERE MARSH-GOBLINS ARE TURN RED AND GOLD TO CINDERS

TASTE SWEET IN THE MOUTH, BUT BURN IN THE BRAIN. WHOEVER EATS THIS ENCHANTED FRUIT

WILL NEVER BE SEEN ON EARTH AGAIN ALL GOBS: HO HO HO HO

GOB: WILL NEVER BE SEEN ON EARTH AGAIN.

THE MARSHELLAISE

KAZOOS MARCH TIME. VOICES

PA PA PA PAH PA PA PA PAH PA PA PA PA PA PAH SQUELCH SQUELCH SQUELCH HERE

COMES THE QUEEN SQUELCH SQUELCH SQUELCH SHE'S REALLY MEAN SLUDGE AND

MUD AND SEEPING OIL ROTTING LEAVES POLLUTED SOIL, IS THE DIET OF THIS

KAZOOS

ROYAL PA PA PAH PA PA PA PAH PA PA PAH PA PA PA PAH PA PAH PA

VOICES

PAH PEOPLE CRINGE AS SHE GOES BY. PERISH CRUMBLE PUTRIFY SQUELCH SQUELCH SQUELCH (SHOUTED)

MARSHESTY BEGUINE

STORYTIME I

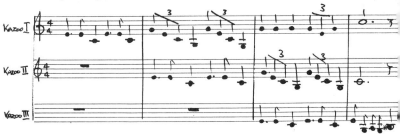

STORYTIME II

LULLABY FOR H.M.

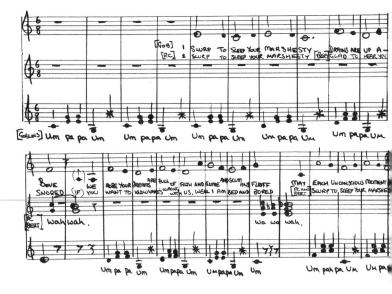

BE EN-TIRE-LY RUBBISH FILLED AND FROM THE SEWER OF YOUR MIND NO PRECIOUS THOUGHT BE
TY, THIS IS YOUR MAT-TRESS WHO'S PUBLIC DUTY IS TO TAKE YOUR NAME AND YOUR ADD-

Wa Wa Wah

Um Um pa pa Um Um
RAL

SPILLED TIL YOU A-WAKEN WAH WAH (End of second verse dissolves into snoring)
RESS, BE CAUSE WE HATE YOU WAH WAH

TIL YOU A-WAKEN WAH WAH

✱ = RASPBERRY NOISE.

MARSHESTY GREETING

voices
unison

Bad mor-ning to your Marshes-ty My word you do look well Bad

mor-ning to your Marshes-ty How horr-i-ble you smell. Oi!

METHUEN PLAYSCRIPTS

If you would like regular information on new Methuen plays,
please write to:
The Marketing Department
Eyre Methuen Ltd
North Way
Andover
Hampshire
England